THE CEO's MINDSET:

*How to **Break Through** to the Next Level*

THE CEO's MINDSET

How to **Break Through** to the Next Level

BEST SELLING AUTHOR

VINNIE FISHER

CEO to the CEOs

The CEO's Mindset:
How to Break Through to the Next Level
by Vinnie Fisher

2680 West Market Street Fairlawn, OH 44333

Published by: A Better You Publishing
Editing by: Ann Maynard & Elaina Robbins
Distributed by: A Better You Publishing
ISBN-13: 978-1532706097
ISBN-10: 153270609X
ISBN-13: 978-0-9909955-3-1
ISBN-10: 0-9909955-3-4
First Edition, 2016
Printed in the United States of America

I dedicate this book to my wife, Debbi. She is my partner for life. She continually is there to help me in operations of life and business. Her dedication to us allows me the privilege to help so many others. She is also continually fighting for the priority of family in our lives. You offer me the greatest opportunity to thrive. I love you very much. Thank you for investing in this journey. God's gift of you in my life has allowed the richness of this book to shine.

My Prayer:

I pray that this book and all that it stands for in our lives is a reminder to help each and every person to be a good steward of the opportunities you have been given. To truly accept the role as a leader in our lives and lead well.

I also pray that each leader is impacted to take the action necessary to thrive. And if this book can help push you into action then please make these words desirable to the reader.

Take the journey today—
You're worth the investment!

Table of Contents

Preface

My name is Vinnie Fisher. I am truly an entrepreneur. I have started, stopped, purchased, sold, scaled, closed, exited, failed and triumphed collectively at over 20 companies that I have created and built in my career.

I have produced a couple hundred million in revenues for multiple companies with over 1,600 employees. So I have had the great privilege and burden of growing multiple 7 and 8 figure businesses.

By profession I am a corporate and tax lawyer who left my law practice to pursue my passion of being an entrepreneur. I tell you all of this to help you understand the context of who is writing this book and why I am writing this book.

To that point, throughout my career, I would constantly see an idea or create one that I believed would offer something great to a bunch of people. I would quickly run down hill and chase my idea. In many cases, I would successfully launch that idea into a business. Then the real journey for me started in the lifecycle of my company.

At first, things are always great regardless of the start. I am always filled with energy in the launch or start-up phase. I carry enough energy for everyone around me. Then I usually get exactly what I set out to conquer: customers and success in sales.

At this point, I would wear multiple hats in the company. And during the start-up phase, you have no choice but to do just that! In my businesses, things would quickly progress. And in less then six months time (in most cases), I would find myself overwhelmed. I needed more people on my team helping me to run and grow this business. I was moving so quickly that I would hire fast without a real purpose or direction for the culture of the company.

Looking back, my strategy of hiring quickly was not the problem. It was the lack of a hiring and firing strategy that actually led to most of my future business struggles.

It takes great people not great systems to take a company to its next level. And as an entrepreneur they are the most important aspect of your company and they require proper strategy and direction for clear execution paramount to any other part of your business.

I feel so strongly about this that I needed to stop my busy life and write this book to help you manage your own mindset; to show you how being in charge of the business you created without having to be in control of every aspect of a business is a real and obtainable goal. And in order for the company to succeed and grow to its next level, you must allow others to control and excel in areas you cannot.

I am an excellent marketer. I love thinking about the sales hook and brand vision for companies and products. I also truly enjoy people and helping them succeed. I like these areas so much that I will ignore other critical areas of our business if it interferes with my desire to work on sales/marketing and the development of other people in our company.

It took me a long time to realize the super powers that I bring to the company — and even longer to understand that I couldn't do it alone. I didn't invest well in the early years of my business career. It took me years to find the mentors and colleagues who would help me refine my process. It took a lot of frustration (and even some financial setbacks) to realize the best positions I should hold in my organizations.

It is truly hard to go at it alone. I am so thankful that I was introduced to a world of personal development. It has allowed me to identify aspects of my talents (or lack thereof) and how those qualities in me impact our organization. As your company grows, one very important step is to get a good understanding of where you ultimately belong. You must realize something at this point: ***The entrepreneur of a business is the "heartbeat" and if the heart is not beating correctly then you are out of rhythm***.

Back to my growth in business, as our company would grow I would quickly hire never truly understanding the open key roles or how to match those roles with the ***"heartbeat"*** of the company. I would hire for competence not culture.

As a result often times I would find myself slowly losing the passion for our business. I became discouraged that

I was trapped in doing things that I didn't want to do and I kept churning through people in the company, causing my key people to also get discouraged and lose drive to push on through the hard times.

Those periods in each of our companies were hard. Our heart was damaged and we were out of rhythm. And you know it could have been avoided. I know one thing you may be considering at this point: the business was probably not working. Well just the opposite, we were bringing in the revenue, well at least the gross. How much we were keeping is an entirely different issue! But more on that issue later.

But what was truly happening was heart disease in our company. We were dying from the inside and we didn't even know it. Well we didn't know how to diagnosis and reverse it in many cases.

Then things changed. As I started to identify the qualities of my talents to our company, I was able to solidify language as to what made me "tick". And it was that identify that started to form the realization that the entrepreneur/owner of a small business is truly its "heartbeat" regardless of the season of its growth. I realized that I can always remain "in charge" of our company as long as I relinquish "control" of certain and specific areas of our business to someone else who will handle it much better than I ever could.

I actually found a way to un-trap myself from our company and bring back the rhythm of our heartbeat. And you can have that too!

That's why I have set-up as my mission to help entrepreneurs get un-trapped from parts of the company. Discover its "heartbeat" and hire and train the key people to help grow and take the organization to its next level.

So a number of years ago I started helping mentor and coach other entrepreneurs on the operation and growth of their companies. During this journey, I help them realize that the mindset of the entrepreneur is critical. Mindset is so important that I had to name the book after it.

The wisdom, techniques and exercises that I bring each entrepreneur throughout our relationship is here in this book. I tried not to hold anything back.

You will discover that information is great. It is critical to strategy. **But without execution and progress you have nothing**. You must develop an **"execution attitude"** and help your team excel in that environment.

I also realized that many other entrepreneurs needed this information and guidance and that I could not help everyone in a one-on-one basis. So I created a few organizations to help (more on that later) and also I decided to write this book to help guide you through the most important part of the company – **you, its "heartbeat"**!

So if you are interested to continue and learn about the entrepreneur mindset and how the CEO of the business should be in charge but not in control of every area of the company in order for it to grow and succeed then this is the book for you.

I will also offer you two ways to interact with this book: (1) just read it in pieces stopping at each exercise and doing them without proceeding until done; or (2) read it twice. The first time straight thru to get the overall vision and concepts and then go back through and do the exercises.

In either case, the exercises are there for you to make progress and develop an "execution attitude" at the highest level. It will also allow you to build momentum. Making progress is one the best kept secrets to momentum. Only the people who put into action the strategy have learned this secret.

Taking action here will also allow you to gain confidence that you actually can be "in charge" of a complete and exceling company and develop great people around you.

I cannot encourage you any more: ***Invest in Yourself! Do it now! You are worth it!*** Get a mentor, join a mastermind, attend workshops and development seminars, and find a coach or consultant who can be there to help you mature and grow in your life and business career. You will never regret that decision.

Note: Throughout this book I will be referring to resources and exercises that you get complete access to at: **www.thetotalceo.com/mindset.**[1]

Introduction

Throughout my career in the business world, I have continually run into leaders, creators, and small business owners who are amazing at providing valuable solutions to meet the needs and wants of their customers. But all too often the business owner is so laser-focused on one facet of his or her company (be it sales, marketing, or product development) the other core areas of the company suffer — even to the point of causing the company and its leader to fail, no matter how great their product or service may be.

Why does this happen? How is it that so many small businesses head down the exact same path of failure, hitting walls and never overcoming them?

Entrepreneurs are constantly developing, creating and distributing products and services that consumers need and want. And as their companies grow, these entrepreneurs are eventually faced with a difficult question: Where do I need to concentrate my energy and attention in order to make my business succeed?

Sadly, the stories of many small businesses in America have a tragic ending. The failure is often due to an owner who kept a single-minded focus for too long, never addressing the other critical areas of the company. Over time his or her business was no longer able to keep the doors open because:

1.   It was not making a profit.
2.   The owner was unable to add other good people to his team.
3.   The owner was unable to manage cash flow for inventory or product expansion.
4.   The owner was spending too much money and not able to withstand the slow periods.
5.   The owner (and therefore the company) veered too far away from the business' original vision.

These and so many other reasons for failure all could have been avoided if the owner invested time, effort and resources into the other essential areas of the business.

And I know this because I have built, grown, and ran a small business very successfully. In fact, I have done it a few times. But sadly, I have also experienced my share of failure because I did not pay attention to my *entire* business.

Thankfully something changed. It was my mindset. I finally became realized that I spent too much effort in sales and marketing — the things I was best at doing — and allowed my lack of focus elsewhere to adversely impact the rest of our business.

As a result of this renewing of my mind, I was finally able to realize that there are six critical areas to a small business. Each area needs attention in order for a business to survive and thrive:

1.   **The Mission:** staying focused on our core mission and operating with an Execution Attitude;

2. **Product/Service:** building the best version of our product or service and then continuing to improve upon it;

3. **Team:** finding and hiring the right people and putting them in the right spots;

4. **Sales and Marketing:** putting your product into the hands of your customers;

5. **Data:** establishing reports to make data-driven decisions and putting good financial measures and systems in place; and

6. **Process:** documenting proper systems in each area of the company in order to keep it running efficiently.

If this message is striking a chord with you, then keep moving along with me. I sincerely promise to you that if you take the time now to invest in yourself, change your mindset, and focus on the tools and techniques to develop an Execution Attitude in your entire company, you will realize growth, profit and happiness that you originally set out to achieve but has been eluding you.

This is not a strategy book. This is an execution book.

Let's take a closer look at what I mean by, "Execution Attitude." For the average entrepreneur, the real problem isn't strategy anyway. We have plenty of strategies. It's easy to put a lot of focus on planning because we're safe there. We feel less likely to fail. It's no surprise then that we can have wonderful strategy sessions, only to walk out and fail to execute. And there lies the core problem this book aims to address: lack of execution.

Do you know Sir Isaac Newton's law of inertia? If I keep something in motion, it's going to remain in motion, right? That's exactly the principle behind one of my mantras: **Progress, not perfection**.

Avoiding stagnation is as simple as making progress every day. Take the list of twelve things you have to do today and boil it down to three. Of those three things, what's the most important one for today? That "most important thing" might take ten minutes, it might take an hour, or it might take a day. Simply identifying it and completing it helps you move forward, and moving forward is addictive. It's consuming. Best of all, it's habitual. The more you move forward every day, the more likely you are to keep moving forward. If you keep reading this book and taking the advice in it, pretty soon you will be skyrocketing in all areas of your life, leadership, and business.

Once you have this attitude of execution, you must apply it to each area of your business in order to have a complete company that is set-up for continued success.

I wrote this book to give you very practical tips that you can use to improve each of the six core areas of your business. I want to help you achieve success by opening your mind and giving you a map to help you along your journey — but it's up to you to take the next forward step, to execute on the advice in these pages.

Let's get started.

Chapter 1

Your Mindset

*"Your first stop will lead to your ultimate
success even if it is the wrong one."*
– Vinnie Fisher

There are six critical areas in each business, but none is more important than the owner's mindset. Each part of the business is built upon the foundation of the vision and perspective of the owner and the executive team. As a business owner, I have personally discovered the impact of the owner's mindset on his or her business and how it can determine the success or failure of a company.

The owner's mindset is so important to the health of your company that if you only read one chapter of this book I want it to be this one.

An owner most often is the creator or founder of an idea, building a great product or service and/or crafting a marketing message that will result in the sale of a good product or service. And in both cases, the owner and the original small team are usually amazing in one or both of these areas. And here is where the business gets its life!

Why is this so bad?

It's not. Actually, without expertise in development and marketing a business will usually not make it through season one. But in order to maintain continued success, a business must address the other four or five critical areas of its company.

This is easier said than done for the owners of any business. Why? Well first off, he or she did not set out to actually run a complete company.

Instead the owner launched a sales campaign and a product or service. This is exactly why so many companies never break through to season two of the business cycle. The mindset of the owner or CEO is focused on sales and growth, not on running a company. And it makes total sense. The owner loves making a sales campaign work but does not want to invest in the operations, systems and back-office of the business. Or the owner may want to make those changes, but he or she doesn't know how so they just don't do it!

I know this because that's me too! I did not want to focus on hiring, data, numbers and systems of the business. I lacked the personal expertise to do it well, and it was much easier for me to create more sales campaigns and funnels than it was to improve my hiring processes or back end systems. My own internal inadequacy and lack of control in these areas of my company made it much easier for me to ignore them than to fix them.

This is where the shift in my mindset came in.

I finally realized that there is more to a company than just marketing and sales. And more important than that, I realized I needed to spend more time in the areas of my business that were outside my wheelhouse — the ones I had been ignoring — in order for my company to succeed.

Now I am not saying that you have to be able to excel in every area of your business in order to succeed. I'm saying you need to know that you cannot do everything. Since you are probably pretty good at sales and marketing, then you need others to help you in the areas of your business you cannot handle. You can be in charge of every area of your business without controlling each one.

This may not be new information to you. The fact that you need others to help you succeed is common knowledge in both business and in life. You probably also know that you're better off focusing on your strengths and delegating your weaknesses. Yes, you might know all of this, but do you have to have the proper mindset to execute on your vision and develop a growth strategy?

Let's take a closer look at the key elements of a healthy CEO mindset.

Determine Your Mission

How can you know where you are going or where you want to go if you do not have a focal point or clearly illuminated path to follow? You can't, right? It's too easy to stumble down the wrong path, burning your time and energy as you move further away from where you want to be. How would you even recognize that you're moving in the wrong direction?

These days, the first thing I ask every client that I work with is to state for me the mission of their company. Almost every one of them fails to do so because the example they offer is unclear or convoluted, or they don't have a mission statement at all.

Mission statements are essential, not only because they keep us on a path toward what we want but they also help us realize when we've made a misstep. A well-crafted and clear mission statement enables you to course-correct before you've strayed too far. It even empowers you to say "no" to something that seems like a great opportunity but may not be a good fit for the company you have created.

If you're thinking, "I already have a mission!" Be very careful. I can't tell you how many times I sit with an entrepreneur and find out that their "completed" mission statement is way off-target. In other words, the company is not on the right path or, worse yet, it's heading in the wrong direction. Missions improve and evolve. It is a living breathing part of your company's life. It should be consistently reviewed and adjusted as needed on an annual basis.

So let's walk through how to come up with your mission and, even more importantly, how to stick to it.

Stop and Do It!

Do you think you already have a strong mission statement for your company? Write it down in only one sentence (two at most). If you cannot clearly convey your company's mission in a sentence or two then your mission is not clear. Follow the steps below to focus your message.

(*If you have an executive team that's larger than just you, I would go through your mission statement together with them. This exercise is wonderful to the development of your company.*)

I have taken many companies through this exercise and I cannot ever remember it being anything short of great for the owner and executive team. Quite frankly, it's usually eye opening for a few reasons:

1. There was no clearly defined mission.
2. The team and owner do not see the mission as the same, and this process creates unity and gets the entire team on the same page.
3. The lack of clarity of mission gives the team an answer as to why the company is all over the place.
4. Once the team sees a clear mission, each member starts to get excited about the vision for the company and attaining the next level of success.
5. With clarity, team members who are "in control" of specific areas of the company have the direction and room to excel!

Your mission is a great place to address the growth, stability and direction of your company because it brings so much clarity. Once you can see clearly then you can easily spot other issues that need to be addressed.

Exercise One: Crafting Your Mission

Go to www.thetotalceo.com/mindset to access our mission creation documents.[2]

Clear away two hours and commit to writing down your core service(s)/product(s) and what you want to accomplish.

Yes, it is that simple!

Once you have a written statement you're happy with, look for ways to trim it down. The strongest mission statements are only one or two sentences long. I have helped in creating many mission statements and one thing has proven true time and time again: the closer to one sentence the clearer the mission. This usually results in a prediction of the success of the company.

I am a true believer in momentum. Once you and your team have a clear vision as to the mission of the company, you will notice that you feel energized and motivated to address other issues in your company — issues that are identified as a result of your clarity. Use this energy to fuel your Execution Attitude!

An Execution Attitude is Crucial

Strategy might help you determine how to adhere to your company's mission, but execution is what will actually move you forward.

This past summer I hired my 14-year-old daughter to

work in our office. I would recommend that every company hire a 14-year-old. The energy in the office is off the charts because of her, and it's actually raising everyone's game a little bit. What is so great about having a teenager at work? She doesn't know enough not to interrupt a meeting. She doesn't have baggage. She's willing to try new things. Most importantly, she'll just *do* whatever she needs to do. Whether she's aware of it or not, my daughter (like most young people) has an execution attitude.

If you were to ask 100 educated professionals, "Are you better at execution or strategy?" all of them would tell you strategy. It's because that's what they've been taught. The average person can create a strategy on how to do something, but they will freeze the moment they actually try to do something. In other words, they get "execution paralysis."

Execution Paralysis

Every day I get calls from people asking for help with their businesses. One of those people, Greg, called me the other day.

Greg was the fourth in command at a very large health company. The company was making $600 million to $1 billion annually selling physical products, information, equipment, and supplements. But while he was enjoying a lot of success there, Greg wanted to make a change.

"I've decided to break away and do things on my own," he told me.

"Good for you," I said. Greg was a highly compensated executive, but I knew that he didn't like the way his big corporation was utilizing him because he didn't feel effective. He felt like middle management, even though he was higher up in the company. He was never going to get more out of his job than he was already; so doing something on his own was his next logical step.

"What are you going to do?" I asked him. "What are you planning?"

"You know, I've spent a lot of time looking at the market, I've spent all these years working with the products we have for our customers. I've done all this studying, all this research and, well, I've realized I really have a passion for health."

> I told him, "Amazing! So which part of it are you going to go after? Are you going to teach? Create informational how-to's from all your years of experience? Did you find some hole in the physical equipment product-space, or some hole in the supplements and food markets?"

"Yes. It's all of them," he replied.

"Okay, so where are you going to start?" I asked.

"Well, that's the thing," he said. "I thought of all this stuff. I have so many things I can do, but I don't know where to start. I'm stuck."

What we have here is a case of execution paralysis, I thought. *This bright, accomplished guy has no idea how to take a step forward toward making his ideas a reality.* It doesn't matter how smart you are or how high up in a company you are — it happens to everyone.

> I told him, "That's very interesting! If you want to actually execute on any of your ideas, you have to pick only one."

He said, "Well, what do you think?"

"I have a lot of thoughts, but which do you believe that you want to start with?"

"Well, I probably think it's best to start with some information."

"Excellent! Information is usually the first thing we can get out because it doesn't require as much fulfillment," I explained. "It usually requires the shortest execution time to get information out into the marketplace and start engaging with your consumers, so I think that is a great idea. What are we going to start with?"

"Well, there are so many different options…"

We went through a lengthy discussion that led him to discovering that he had hundreds of education ideas. He was over-aware and spent too much time analyzing the market. For all his strategies, he had no outline for execution.

Start with "How"

"How am I going to do it" is the quantum leap in business, the giant gap between strategy and execution. A great quote I enjoy saying to my team is one I picked up from 37 Signals.[3] It goes something like this: "The longer it takes to develop, the less likely it will launch or deploy."

Execution paralysis comes back to a core emotion: fear of failure. Strategy, ironically, is one of the primers to this emotion. The better we develop and plan out how it's going to work, the more our strategy kicks up our fear. We start looking at what we have to do to execute with excellence, and we get overwhelmed. We don't want the first step to be a wrong one, so we don't take one at all! Or worse, we're afraid that if our first step isn't perfect it will lead to disaster. It's just the opposite actually. The first step will lead to your ultimate success *even if it's the wrong one.* Taking action, not over-planning, is the key to ultimate success.

That is why getting your company aligned with its core mission will not only give you vision, it will also prime your Execution Attitude. And as you take action toward fulfilling your company mission, you will create momentum in your business.

Avoid Gap Lies

Overemphasis on strategy and the inability to execute is a core problem that exists throughout all sectors, industries, and success levels. People hate executing so much that they actually lie to themselves to avoid crossing from strategy to execution. I call these "gap lies," and it's essential to the owner's mindset to recognize these pitfalls and avoid them. Here are a few of my favorites:

Money: "If I had money, I could act on my idea and make a fortune." If this were true, how many of the greatest entrepreneurs would never have succeeded?

Team: "If I only had the right people on the team..." The right team doesn't just jump into your lap; you have to build it.

Expertise: "I just don't know enough about that subject." If you have an original idea for a product, *no one* knows enough about it. You have to become the expert.

Demand: "How do I know that the consumer really wants what I'm selling?" There's some truth to this one, but how will you ever know unless you try giving it to them? How can you adapt if you can't get feedback?

Complete Product: "I need to have every detail figured out and completed before I sell it to the marketplace." This one is so dangerous that it kills most people!

These core foundational lies are the major reason why people just don't execute. It's not something that's reserved to the solo-preneur or the young entrepreneur who's just getting started. It's at every level of the workforce in every organization regardless of its size.

Fortunately, there is an age where this execution paralysis still hasn't taken hold — and that brings me back to my 14-year-old new-hire.

In my office, we have struggled to find a quality video person to edit videos that we feature in some of our educational materials. That's why we hired my daughter. Like every 14-year-old, she wants to be a superstar on YouTube. She also has the skill and creative ability to play with the software and technology involved in creating online videos.

Three weeks into the hire, she was already executing at a very high level. We'd give her a step to take, and she'd do it without a second thought. She doesn't have all these fear gaps in place. She's just executing. And so can you.

You do not need to have amazing domain expertise to be a manager. You have to be taught some of the disciplines of execution to be a good manager, but expertise in some specific topic isn't necessary. We're proving that with my daughter, who is now executing better than people twice, three times, even four times her age. At some point, we may need to start pushing out a series of videos and she will probably become our video department.

Developing a mindset that is focused on progress not perfection is critical to growing expertise. I will talk about expertise in great detail in the hiring section of this book but the principle applies to you as the entrepreneur as well. You weren't an expert in what ever you claim to be an expert in until you became one! That's the point, its developed not magically created.

So I encourage you to act like a 14 year old and have a "go for it" mindset! As you continue down your path you will get smarter, gain more wisdom and further develop your expertise.

This is very important to the entrepreneur/owner who, like me, has avoided the complete operations of the business due to the fact that he or she is inadequate and doesn't know how to do it. I am here to tell you that you can do it and it starts with trying not denying.

Try and Try Again

Here's the underlying strategy people normally have: You've got to have the whole thing figured out before you execute. You don't want to come out of the box immature or incomplete, because you don't want people to think you're incompetent or underdeveloped.

This thinking is all wrong. People would rather know you're trying to improve than believe you have it all together.

Execution is about moving and having the ability to stop and see what happened. It's an experimental process. The reason I have been so successful in business is because I've taken a more scientific approach to execution. Think back to high school science class. Do you remember learning how to formulate a hypothesis? Treat your strategy the same way you would a simple hypothesis. What do you think consumers want? What type of person do you

want around the office? What do you enjoy doing? Don't make it any more complicated than that.

And what did you do in science class once you had a hypothesis? You started experimenting to test it, right? So experiment! Test a promotion or put a short video together, interview people, try out a solution in a certain area of your business. With the technology of today, we shouldn't be mired in the long outline process of preparing to try something.

In marketing and sales this is never truer. What I've learned in business is to try little pieces of the idea instead of over-developing it and having it turn out to be no good. Bad ideas can be 100% bad for business, but maybe customers actually like a small 10% of it that you can use to grow a better business. You won't know until you're in the field or have personally tried the product you're giving the consumer.

One day the COO at my CFO-outsourcing company, Fully Accountable™, came to me and said, "I've got this really good idea."

I said, "Great! Tell me about it. What is it?"

"I'd like to create a HR compliance department. Every one of our clients is coming to us and saying that they have high-level HR needs, so they can't deal with hiring and training their new people. All the way from identifying role in the company, recruiting, ads for hire, interviewing and training the new hire — they're always asking if we have stuff for them. There's definitely a demand for this kind of service, we just don't know where to start it."

I gave her one bit of advice that I give my clients all the time: "Let's start with the simplest thing you can do. What's the one thing our customers are asking for when it comes to their HR needs?"

"They have a hard time finding new team members," she said.

"So instead of developing a super-amazing plan, let's call one of our clients and tell them we're going to help them find that person. Let's help them do exactly what we do to find our own people and see how it goes. If we incubate this idea with one or two external clients, we'll find out what we want to deliver and what they want delivered to them."

Fully Accountable's ™ mission is not HR related, so a different team would have to develop this idea. And that is what happened: the hypothesis was tested and a new company was created. Today, that company is launched and has developed its workshops and materials to help entrepreneurs' hire and train people on their team. This is only because they started taking steps. They started doing something small, which allowed them to play with their idea. You can learn more about this process and the story of the company's development at: www.thetotalceo.com/mindset.

The 70% Rule — It's all mindset

Earlier in my career, I had a realization that was a very big deal for me: a 70% version of me was good enough.

I learned this lesson from a gentleman I worked with

when I was a practicing lawyer. He was an immigrant who owned factories here in the U.S. I was on a plane with him to visit his factories and go through some production compliance items — ordinary corporate lawyer tasks with which he wanted me involved.[4]

We were leaving one of the plants in a golf cart, driving back to the runway, when I said, "You know, that guy did things a little differently than I would have expected you to do them. Are you sure you're okay with that?" He stopped the golf cart so fast he nearly gave me whiplash.

"Listen," he said, "I want to give you a really important lesson, and you're going to need to take this with you in order to be successful in growing your firm. If you believe you're going to completely duplicate yourself, then you're going to have an impossibly high standard. No one will ever live up to that standard. You're going to churn people up, or worse than that, you're never going to take any chances on expanding your ideas or your thoughts."

He started the golf cart back up again and didn't say another word. I thought what he said was interesting, but I didn't know what to do with it.

Back at the office, I worked for a partner of a big firm and I was progressing quickly in my career. There was, however, one little thing that bothered me. I would hand my boss a document and he would change the wording for no reason. He was an excellent lawyer, but he was also a control freak. His practice was no better for it. It certainly wasn't growing.

It wasn't until years later, when I was running a business of my own, that I started connecting the dots. I was a control freak too (like most entrepreneurs, including yourself) and, like my boss at the law firm, my impossibly high standard was standing in the way of my company's growth.

As idea creators, we have so much passion and we want things done a certain way. When we train our managers to think and work under that rubric, they think they need to be another version of you; and so they start thinking — unbeknownst to you — "Would Vinnie do it that way? I should just wait for his opinion because he probably has this figured out." They are no longer free thinkers; they are merely executors of your thoughts and directives. They become micromanaged people. They resolve themselves to being broken into a job they don't want to do, become miserable and move on; or they stop being effective because they no longer *feel* effective.

That's why in my office we say, "You've got to be okay with 70% of yourself." I decided to change my mindset about who was able to do a certain job. I realized that if I couldn't accept somebody doing things a little different than me, I was never going to grow. I would stifle progress by controlling anything that veered from what I expected, or run off something or someone because it did not meet my personal high standard. I realized it's okay for someone to do something a little different (or a little worse) than you'd do yourself. Once you grasp that concept, you start allowing people freedom to do tasks in their own way.

Letting go gave me the ability to start focusing on core things, like the three important things in my company: mission, values, and principles. As long as work is executed on that core, it can be done a little differently than I would do it personally. This allowed us to expand through managers who have the freedom to lead in their own way instead of trying to be just like me.

That critical shift in my mindset allowed us to grow. Without that change, our business would be completely dependent on me and it would never have a chance of becoming a great company.

Conclusion

The entrepreneur who is the CEO of the company is the creator and director of the business. It's your mindset that will determine the direction of the company.

You must develop a renewing of your mind. A mind set on the following principles:

- An understanding that you cannot do everything on your own.
- You must have a clear mission for your company; one you can communicate simply.
- You must have an Execution Attitude, and infuse it into your company's culture.
- Stay focused on progress, not perfection.
- People are more important that systems. (We will discuss this in the next chapter.)
- You must be able to accept a 70% version of yourself.

- Remember: a company is bigger than one person. You must have great people on your team in order to excel. And those great people must be "in control" of areas you cannot handle.

By getting these elements set, you will have created a healthy foundation for your mindset and be better positioned to tackle the other crucial areas of your company.

Resources:

1. **Identify your talents.** We have exercises posted at www.thetotalceo.com/mindset.[5]

2. **Don't forget to create your mission!** You can find Fully Accountable's™ mission statement at www.thetotalceo.com/mindset.[6]

3. **Learn more about what we're doing!** You can learn more about Fully Accountable™ at www.fullyaccountable.com.[7]

Chapter 2

People

*"Finding your 'heartbeat' allows you
to hire for culture over competence."*
–Vinnie Fisher

The evolution of your company starts with you creating a product or service and figuring out the right sales message to create orders. It's at this point when your company has its greatest level of service and cheapest cost of delivery. Then things have to change. You realize that you cannot do it alone (usually by being too busy, not through self-awareness) and you start hiring people to join your team. This is when things really get interesting.

An owner simply cannot handle everything. A growing business needs people on the team in order to maintain an acceptable level of service. But that's often easier said than done. Almost every client of mine has major issues hiring the right people to be on the team. There are several factors that lead to this problem but, as you already know, it likely stems from the fact that the business owner is not a hiring expert. So what happens? The owner makes hiring decisions based on a bunch of false assumptions and is then discouraged when the hires don't work out.

This brings us to the next most important key to operating a successful company: you've got to have the right people serving in the right places.

I want to address one issue at this point: I do believe that a business must have a good product or service in order to survive the long haul as a company. But my expertise is in working with existing companies. And the obvious assumption that must be made is that an operating company has at least a minimally viable product or service in order to be an active operating company taking sales. So while a product or service is important and one can always be improved, an operating company must have good people serving in the right places in order to address all of the other areas of the company. That's what makes this chapter so important.

Looking For the Right People

I like what author Jim Collins has to say about priorities: Would you rather have a broken-down bus filled with a bunch of mechanics, or a pristine bus filled with four-year-olds?[8] Lots of CEOs focus on the bells and whistles instead of what is really important: personnel. The CEO's most important job is acquiring team members. If the CEO does not have personnel as their number one priority, then growth is going to be a major problem for the company.

What will happen to your company if you take someone who doesn't believe in or understand your company mission and put them in charge? Whatever it is, it won't be good. You can always have somebody put systems in place, but if your people aren't in line with the mission, your systems won't count for much. In other words, if your pristine bus full of toddlers breaks down, your trip is over.

The first part of execution is establishing a team, and that starts with a mindset that believes in people over systems. Once you are there, you need to identify your mission and values so you can find the right people.

Your Mission

As you continue to grow your team this exercise is critical. As I presented earlier, your mission is critical for the success of your company. It is also critical for the acquisition and development of your team. You need to state your mission to prospects and existing team members. Each person must be on the same path, going in the same direction.

Important point: Make sure you have already completed the mission exercise from the previous chapter. Confirm you are on the right path and heading in the right direction. This is critical to casting vision to your current people and acquiring talented people to join the team.

Core Values

The hiring process should not be a guessing game. In fact, there should be no guesswork involved at all. I have conducted thousands of interviews and had over

1,600 employees during my career. How can you expect someone to stay on the team if he or she does not line up with your core values? Have you even defined your core values? If you haven't, then it's time to do so.

Defining your core values is actually an amazingly wonderful and powerful exercise for your business. In order to help you understand the importance of your core values, I'll explain the process of determining your core values and give some examples as to how it works. But first, let's look at some of the most common hiring mistakes business owners make.

Personnel issues typically stem from the fact that we often hire for competence instead of culture. The problem with this style of hiring is that it often results in onboarding a new-hire whose core base of values do not line up with you and your executive team. I have been guilty of doing this so many times.

I recall one time we were looking for someone to join our programming team. I met with one young man and watched as he easily passed our competency-programming test. Then he passed our first interview with flying colors. I met with him again on his second interview and he explained to me his ability to handle any code language and how he was a fast learner.

I started to get real excited about his skills. Actually I got so excited that I did not spend any time looking into any red flags or issues that he may have had in keeping a job with our company. We offered him the role, and he accepted. The wheels fell off almost immediately after he started.

His lack of commitment to the job started to show right away. He was often late, sloppy in his code, and short with fellow team members. Within a few weeks he was terminated from the company. So what happened? Despite his strong coding skills, this young man did not have a chance of succeeding in our company. He did not represent any of our core values. We went back and evaluated him on his character and were able to determine that he should not have been hired.

We not only wasted our time in bringing him on, but we caused disruption to the entire team by having him in the company even for this short time. So how could this have been avoided?

In order to acquire good team members you need to have a gauge with which to properly evaluate people.

Finding Your Heartbeat!

I told you we would come back to this concept of the "heartbeat" of the company and how that's you! Your core values are your best tool for evaluating people. I know what you are thinking: so how do I figure out our core values? I recommend you do the following:

1. Write down between 10-15 values that describe you and your executive team (if it's just you, that's fine). No need to define them yet. Just write the words.

2. Share those terms with your executive team and ask them each to pick five from the list. Also allow them to have a write-in if they feel strongly about anything that is not on the list. Be sure to pick your own five as well.

3. Meet with the executive team and have each person state their five terms plus their reasons for selecting them.

4. Compile the list, confirm the ones you all agree upon, and work through any disagreement until you mutually agree on your company's five core values.[9]

There is something amazing that happens when executive teams are placed together correctly. I have observed over and over again that, without looking at each other's lists, a well-aligned team will already agree on at least three of the five choices from the list. In many cases, it's 4 or, in truly fun cases, 5 of them. It's amazing but it happens every time.

(Note: There may be outliers — and more on that issue in a moment — and it may mean that they do not belong on the team.)

Not too long ago, I did this exercise with the executive team at my company, Fully Accountable™. We followed the steps above to figure out our core values. And I knew what was going to happen for the four of us — we lined up on all five of our core values: Intelligent, Reliable, Caring, Honesty and Commitment. It was a great day, filled with lots of energy and vision as we defined the things that mattered most and found ways to implement them within the company. We also walked out of the room knowing we had the right executive team on the bus.

Determining your values is actually identifying the "heartbeat" of your company. And it's this 'heartbeat" that you must exercise, treat and care for consistently; because if the heart beats out of rhythm the heart will take on damage and ultimately die. This brings us to the concept of Reverse Hiring™.

With these values in hand, your interviewing should be consistent as you determine if someone is a good fit for your team. I would first recommend evaluating your existing team, including your executive team, to see how each of you scores on your values.

I have learned over so many employees that values alignment is a clear indicator of a team member's success in the company. When employees match three or more values, he or she has an overwhelming success rate. The opposite is also true. When team members share two or fewer core values, then that team member should not be on the team. And probably won't be for very long.

Recently we hired a new team member and our HR director came up to me and said, "I am really excited about our new person, she scored 5 out of 5 for our core values!" And guess what? She is an amazing member of the team today!

Hiring Through a "NO" standard

The key to the Reverse Hiring™ technique is to use your core values as a shield against hiring someone. So it goes like this:

1. Identify a needed role in the company;
2. Select candidates based on expertise and experience;
3. Test candidates' job qualifications before any extensive interview; and
4. Use core values as your shield to look for a "no" with qualified people.

In the resource section, I prepared the perfect interview sheet. You can also find a link at www.thetotalceo.com/mindest for the perfect interview.[10]

With the idea of how to hire the right people, we need to spend time on identifying spots that need to be filled on the team.

Growing Your Business the Right Way

As an entrepreneur, understand that you can't do everything on your own. Internalize that knowledge before you go out and start hiring a team. Otherwise you'll hire the wrong people. Earlier in my career, I hired people exactly like myself. I thought I really needed another person who could get things done like I do. In reality, I needed to create a team of people who could perform tasks I was not good at doing. They would be the ones who proved critical to the success of the company.

Before you start hiring, you have to do an inventory assessment of what you need. In my case, I am excellent at taking an idea and bringing it to life. I'm not good at integration, organization and following through on details.

For your first hire, go out and find someone who fills in a weakness or need in your business that you would not be inclined to do yourself. Instead of trying to get better at it, you should surround yourself with people who can complement you in your business. You can't execute as a team unless you have the right people focusing on the right details.

> **Try the following exercise**: Sit down and think about what you're not good at, what you want to accomplish, and why you should add someone to the team to accomplish the task. Prioritize the list based on the most important holes for that season of your business.

The Key Three People Needed in Any Business

I've noticed that good things tend to come in threes. There are three fundamental people who are critical to a company's success:

1. The entrepreneur/creator. The owner or founder is usually this person. But a marketer or department leader can often be in this role.

2. The technical person.
3. The manager.

Those are very distinct functions in a company, and a solo-preneur has no choice but to be all three. But that should not be the case in a small business staffed with more than just the founder.

Personally, I would never start a company with less than three people. Some people have to start out with less, but ideally you would have an owner, a technician, and a manager. And entrepreneur/creator should be working on the acquisition of revenue, not on the completion of tasks. The technician needs to complete the items necessary for fulfillment of the product for delivery. The manager needs to make sure that the vision is correctly implemented.

Entrepreneur/Creator: The creator or inventor is usually the entrepreneur (not exclusively, but usually). Not all owners are creators, of course. You may have partnered up or rode up the coattails of creativity, which is fine. Not all leaders are inventors, but you have to quickly decide your role in the company and grow with it.

Technician: The next piece is your technician. I used to believe that you must have all your technicians in your office, but the advancement of technology has dictated otherwise. Technicians can be anywhere. They need to be competent and capable of doing their work, but the idea of managing their work is another issue.

Technicians require a different approach than managers. Though he or she usually wants to produce the product or service requested, you can't always push a technician because he or she might shut down on you. This is where the manager really helps with the process.

Manager: A manager is the common denominator. He or she frees up the inventor and the technician to do their jobs, and makes sure their work is implemented. The technician and inventor don't roll up to the manager; instead the manager is there to serve the technician and inventor by making sure all three parts of the business are correctly done. The manager is in control of the integration of vision.

A lot of companies have the wrong management attitude, and it probably has something to do with the way we are as humans. We think of our place in the herd and over time, the smartest people rise to become the executive staff. The executive staff becomes managers and they sit around and tell people what to do. The company becomes manager-driven and inefficient, as opposed to a creative and technically driven company.

We, on the other hand, train for project managers, and their job is to make sure the technician and the inventor or creator or marketer — whatever word you want to put there — has their voice heard and their work completed on time. We have a formula for this:

Vision   Technical   Manager's Job
(Implementation)

Size Matters

Paul Graham (venture capitalist, programmer, and founder of the incubator Y Combinator) was asked in a *Techcrunch* interview a few years ago why he invested in single-founder companies.[11] He said that only 1 in 1,000 make it, and only one of his single-founder investments proved successful: Dropbox. And even in that case, they worked quickly to get him an executive team in place.

Going at it alone is significantly harder than working with a team, and it makes a company less likely to succeed. It's extremely hard to go at it alone with no one to collaborate. Dropbox was a rare circumstance; Paul got burned every other time he invested in solo projects. Y Combinator now has a regular policy not to invest in single-founder companies, and I understand why. It's the same reason why I ask anyone coming to me for business advice: "Is it just you, or is your partner involved?" If there is no partner, I quickly follow up with: "Are you bringing someone else on the team?"

I'm not saying your business has to be a 50/50 investment with someone else, but you have to create "entre leaders" in your business. If you create a company alone and you want to grow a team, where is the opportunity for another person to join? At the incubator level, I get why they want more than one founder (usually it takes a lot effort and it's pre-revenue), but you can take that exact principle and move it into any business and the results are the same.

If you're in a small organization where you have to wear two hats, make sure you don't wear three of them. If you do, then you're not a business; you're a solopreneur. If you stop working, there is no business. A manager is supposed to make sure that work gets completed. He or she is responsible for removing barriers that allow completion of projects. If that manager is also wearing a technician's hat, their job gets a little harder because they have to manage and prioritize their work. If they're also the creator, then they manage, prioritize, and feel like they have to do everything. It's a totally different dynamic.

Get the Right People Doing the Right Things: Project and Process People

Hire the right people and put them in the right places to make sure they can execute properly.

I always say, "We're hiring for Rachel," in our office. It's a term we use for finding someone who has a good attitude, great effort, and the right ability to learn. It all comes from Rachel, who is an actual person who works for me.

When Rachel first joined us, she didn't know a lot about our business. She came in as a law clerk and I quickly realized she had very good process ability. I learned she was tenacious, with a great attitude and the ability to follow through. Fast forward a few years and she was on our team, accomplishing things like crazy. Everyone loved her.

But then something changed. She was so competent that everyone starts giving her more and more work. Over time, Rachel's performance started suffering in some areas. We were left asking, "What happened to Rachel? She used to be so good."

It was then that the figurative light bulb went on for us. We knew we had to fix the situation very quickly, but we also learned something we still use at a higher level.

Let me break it down. In a work environment, there are two types of people. Despite your attitude, effort, and ability, you are either a *project-type* person or a *process-type* person.

Project People

A project person likes to take on new initiatives. They may not have a direction or vision, but they can be in charge of completing one. They can complete that project, but when they're done, they don't want to do it again. They always want to start on the next thing. To a project person, doing a repetitive task is like watching paint dry.

Project people like consistency, but their consistency is variety. To them, discovering and building new ideas is life.

Project people thrive in sales because they don't sell someone the exact same way every time. Marketing people are also more project-oriented because they need to change and craft their message constantly. Writers, typically creative writers and copywriters, have more project-based mindsets because it's a new subject every time. Lawyers who are litigators have a more project attitude because they become experts on a subject just for one trial before they move on to something else.

If you're a creative writer, you probably don't want to be the person doing the transcription every day. Just as you wouldn't muzzle an ox, you wouldn't take a writer and say, "Oh you're awesome! So why don't you do our transcription, because we need to get that done."

But that's what businesses do. They say, "You know what? You're so good at that you've got to be good at this. So, can you do this too?" We call it the "pile-on list" and before you know it, the writer has 45 tasks to do and they only like doing 2 or 3 of them. Then we start wondering, what happened to that writer? Why did they fizzle out?

I'm personally a good example of this. I have the amazing ability to create vision and execute an idea, but then I reach a point where I can't continue to run daily operations. It's just within my makeup. It's so much in my makeup that if left to my own devices, I will break something just to tinker with it. I am through-and-through a project person, so much so that we've had to put a failsafe for when a job goes from project to process. We make sure to get me out of the way because I will break it.

Process People

A process person rarely likes coming up with an idea and isn't comfortable being the one figuring something out. However, if you hand them an outline with 27 steps, not only will that outline grow to 35 steps, it'll be better.

A process person's complete joy in life is to do the same tasks over and over, and do them more efficiently each time. To a process person, being an innovator or a creator is so overwhelming that they shut down. Incidentally, doing the same tasks daily and improving upon them is new and innovative to a process-type person.

When I was a kid, there was a company called GTE, and their tagline in a commercial was, "We don't make things, we just make things that people want better."[12] I thought that was a cool tagline. There are people who don't want to be charged with the responsibility of coming up with a new headline. If you want them to run a campaign and know the statistics, learn your opt-in rate and your engagement rate, they'll be amazing at it — but don't ask them to come up with the marketing collateral.

This is not to say that process people aren't creative. When a process person feels creative in the world that they're in, they thrive. They feel like they have freedom, and we don't stifle that. We just make sure we treat it correctly by making sure it's not their responsibility outside their creativity zone.

There is a wonderful person in my company who maintains our merchant accounts. She's an excellent, detail-oriented micro manager who can process like nobody's business. You tell her what to do, and she does it. But the second she has to start with an idea to do something, she shuts down. She thrives on her process job of doing the applications, managing the GAA, understanding chargebacks, retrievals and refunds, talking to the banks, making sure there's enough money, and our deposits are coming in when they're supposed to arrive.

When she's managing all of that excellently, something interesting happens. She starts having great ideas. We love that, but no matter how many great ideas she has and no matter how many of her ideas we implement, we won't make creating them her job responsibility outside of her creativity zone. She doesn't want that kind of pressure; plus, the minute she feels required to come up with new ideas, she will stop generating them.

Hybrids

Can you be both? Yes, I believe so. We have one in our office: Rachel! She's an amazing person who can up with ideas, but she does not want to be the one who creates the big picture. She falls short of vision, but the second she sees it, she can grab it quickly and run with it. She also falls a little short of wanting to do the exact repetitive thing every day. She's basically somewhere in the middle.

What we have to do is make sure we've given her enough of the vision so that she can execute. We also make sure we don't stick her in the job that's repetitive every day.

The polarized ones are the easiest to place. With someone who's straight up process or project, like me, you know what to do with him or her. The hybrids can be tougher to place in the right spot, but when you do... watch out. It's the Rachel's of the world who, if used correctly, are the true agents of change.

Hiring great people and putting them in the wrong spot or letting them drift away from the core spot they hold, is just as bad as not understanding there are different personality types for each persona and role in our companies.

The Consequences of Ignoring Personality Types

We tend to hire people for attitude and effort and then stick them with the wrong assignments for their personality. For example, is a project person the right fit for a role doing bank reconciliations day in and day out? Would you be maximizing his or her talents by jamming them into the accounting department?

I once inadvertently asked a process person to do work suitable for a project person, and I lost an amazing content writer because of my request. She's still a friend of mine and she was a wonderful writer, probably one of the best I've hired. She had some attitude issues and she knew it, but she had amazing process abilities. If you handed her something, she'd find the flaw in the process and make it better.

When we had our publishing business, I made the gigantic mistake of putting her in charge of the content department. She suddenly had to come up with ideas for the marketing and management of the content. She fizzled and became the worst employee I had within 90 days. After working with us for over seven years, she went from hero to zero in an instant. It was 100% my fault. That's what happens when you put great people in bad spots.

When these things happen, we tend to ask the wrong questions because we aren't aware of the core things that are important to a team member. We say, "I wonder what's going on in her personal life," or, "Something is distracting her, what could it be?" or, "What changed that is causing her to perform like this? She must be looking for another job." We don't ask what *we* did to change her job and crush her performance. We always blame external factors.

I've had over 1,600 employees, and I think of the proverbial funerals we've had, many of them self-inflicted. We had so many quality people on the team whom we then placed in the wrong spot. Had we fixed that along the way, we would have saved a lot of job funerals and kept a lot of great talent.

Putting someone in the right spot is critical, and one of the best ways of finding their right spot is to ask them. Just ask them, "Are you a project-person or are you a process-person?" Since he or she probably hasn't heard the title before you may have to expand: "Do you like to come up with the ideas or do you like to take someone's idea and make it better?" You will be amazed at the results of talking with your people.

When you place the right person in the right spot and the environment is an execution environment, these correctly positioned people tend to thrive.

Execution is Everyone's Problem

It can be tempting, but we shouldn't assign stereotypes to project and process people when it comes to execution. It's a problem for everybody. Project people have focus problems. They often have a bunch of great ideas and want to chase ten of them at the same time, and because of that, they don't execute even one of them well. They might have some inherent ability to execute, but they're completely scattered. That's usually the project-person's biggest Achilles' heel.

A process person's execution issues stem from the responsibility of coming up with the idea and fear of failure. The process person will say, "What do you mean I have to come up with the next way to do this?" It feels too big and overwhelming. This is a true execution killer. The second we break down the large idea into actionable pieces, they perform and usually very well.

If I asked everyone on my team to write me a letter detailing what he or she does at their job, guess who would be done first? That's right, the process people. The systems of a process person are usually far greater than a project person's. Their execution of tasks depends on the type of work they're given.

> **Try the following exercise:** Set up a meeting with your direct reports and ask them about whether he or she is a project or process-type person. Also ask them if they believe they are doing the right job for the company.

Oh, and in the end, Rachel never fizzled out because we caught our mistake. But if we hadn't taken precautions, the situation could have ended much differently. Though she had barely any experience in business and working in a corporate environment when we hired her, Rachel had the right core values that matched my "heartbeat". She also had a great attitude, exhibited excellent ability and was willing to put in unquestioned effort. She has since been homegrown into a core business partner in the company.

Homegrown Experts

Whether I'm at a conference taking questions from a big group, or reading a post on a private forum, I often see the same sentiment from entrepreneurs. They'll say something like: "I'm looking to hire a media strategist who is the top of the business at doing advertising. I want to have them come on to our team. We'll hire them on an external basis, but they'll be part of our team. We want only the best."

Here's the problem: they have no idea who the best is! *"The best" will have a different meaning for each company is actually different because we should be hiring (employees or vendors) for culture not competence.*

As entrepreneurs, we're so used to skipping to the front of the line for things we want. We have the same attitude when growing our internal or external teams. We hire for competence, not character. If we were really honest with ourselves, then what we want is an amazing programmer that can execute and accomplish what we want. We don't think about if that person will mesh with our ideologies or share our values. (As an aside, if you hire with your core values as a gauge then you can virtually eliminate this issue).

Even in the execution of building the right team, we start with the strategic presumptions about how we want to build our team. We've even strategized the right ways of hiring! We *think* because we don't know what to *do*. Instead of taking the time to develop a person into the expert we need, we presume we've got to have the expert on the team right *now*.

The expert that you are working so hard to find didn't even know how to do that job before they became an expert. My teenager is not an expert at YouTube, she's not an expert at videos, but guess what she's going to end up becoming? — An expert at both. We're going to continue to put that product out there and continue to improve upon it, and that's how you build an army of execution disciples. You should train the disciples instead of worrying about bringing competence to the table. Competence is a bonus; it shouldn't be a prerequisite.

In searching for the right fit on your team: (1) you have identified a core need that rises to the level of a job opening; (2) you have the heartbeat of the company; and (3) you are looking for someone with the requisite skill set to do the job. Sounds easy, right? If it is that easy, what goes wrong? Well, quite frankly the entrepreneur usually doesn't handle the three items above. But with those in hand, we have learned not to over compensate on expertise but rather on the effort, ability and attitude of any candidate to fit into our environment. This is not a one size fits all for every company. But when executed correctly all companies that do it thrives!

The Triangle Offense

Developing your team comes down to another set of threes: attitude, effort, and ability.

Attitude: People come in with the attitude that they have. They'll be exactly who they are and, depending on the environment, they're either going to thrive or not. This is why it is so essential that their character and values align with the mission and core values of the company. Our job is not to force them into our environment because they have some ability that we want. Our job is to make sure they are the right fit; because that's the only way their competence is going to shine.

Effort: If someone isn't willing to try hard and give something their all, they will not be successful. You want your workers to put in 100% effort naturally so you can trust them to do their work. You also want people who put in effort for results not credit.

Ability: The final piece is ability. Someone has to be able to do the job. If you need a lawyer, you can't hire someone who hasn't passed the bar. There are many cases where people can pick up new skills and become experts, but pre-qualified individuals will better meet the needs of roles that require special licensing or acumen.

Good teams do not happen by accident. During the hiring process, be sure to remember the Triangle: attitude, ability, and effort. This is your offense in hiring and along with your mission you can clearly lay out the vision of your company to a qualified candidate. But don't forget, your defense is the shield of your core values and applying Reverse Hiring™ in shopping for "No" as the way to avoid competence over culture hiring.

The Leader and The Mission

When I'm sitting in an interview, most of the time my role is to be the one who speaks about the mission of our business. I look for someone who shares the mission of what we're trying to accomplish. I'm always talking about mission and our particular values because, no matter what, the organizational culture is defined top-down (the "heartbeat"). I set what the standard has to be.

As the leader of your company, you must clearly demonstrate your adherence to your mission while also making sure that your team buys into it. We've learned you are more likely to work through the rough patches, the growth, and the hard stuff when everyone is on the same page from the very beginning.

The Triangle Hierarchy

Of the three points of the triangle (effort, attitude and ability), which one do you think is the most important? If you said ability, you are not alone...but you might want to reconsider your position.

At my company, we hire for attitude, followed by effort and lastly ability. Ability is important, but it has nothing to do with competence. If you don't have the right attitude, or if you're not willing to put in the effort, it doesn't matter how capable you are at the job. When doing interviews, we completely stop moving forward with an applicant if we find that their attitude doesn't fit with our company.

Prescreen for Ability

It may seem counterintuitive to hire for attitude over ability, especially for jobs that are technical, like programming, graphic design, accounting and others where the focus is on the final result. However, ability is a very easy thing for which you can solve. The vast majority of your applicants will be qualified, and if they aren't, you can weed them out with a quick pre-screening test before moving on to effort and attitude.

In order to become a lawyer, for example, you must pass the bar exam. In order to be a doctor you have to have a medical license. If you need to hire a doctor or a lawyer, you can assume that they have the ability to perform as long as they have those core certifications.

With other professions that do not require degrees, things get a little more complicated. Programmers, for example, don't have to take a test to become licensed. So before you start testing their effort and attitude, you have to test their ability.

Let's say you have one hundred programmers you're considering.   First, ask them ten technical questions. Make that the first thing you do before proceeding with the interview. That way, if ninety fail and only ten pass, you know those ten are technically competent and suitable for the position.

In our companies and with our clients, we use skill tests for our accountants, programmers and even managers that check for technical competence in a certain position. If an applicant passes the test then we move them on to the interview process, which is specially designed to focus on attitude. If he or she has the right attitude, we'll invite them to an in-person interview where we focus on both attitude and effort.

The Right Attitude

As an owner or entrepreneur, you have to decide the most important things you are culturally fighting for, and that becomes the definition of the attitude you're shopping for in your prospective hires. Here are three of the things I look for in my candidates:

Self-Awareness: The first thing to search for in a candidate is self-awareness. It's critical because if they don't have it then training them through their limitations and building on their strengths will be much harder.

Self-Introspection: The second quality to look for is self-introspection. A candidate has to look internally when dealing with failure. They should not finger-point at external factors.

Team Spirit: Third, they have to thrive in a team environment and they shouldn't want to go at it alone. People who want to do things alone don't belong on a team. Don't bring them into your environment because they'll never truly fit in.

Depending on the job, a key core attitude is the desire to perform as a team player. Look for someone who doesn't want to shine alone. It's a particularly big deal in sales departments because most sales people want to be lone wolves. So how do you find somebody who has the attitude to be a team player?

We know we need somebody who's willing to be there and help pick up team members who fall and fail. That's a big deal in our environment. We run our questions through those filters and shop for a team player with that personality. (You can go to www.thetotalceo.com/mindset for more information and resources on hiring.)[13]

Integrity: Never allow for conversation about other people that is not neutral or positive. We don't allow negative conversation about someone else unless it's spoken directly to him or her. In other words, we don't believe in gossip. If you have that habit, we weed it out immediately or the person leaves the team.

Ask questions about conflicts candidates have had in their previous workplace. Make them explain it to you. We're not shopping for positive things; we're shopping for things that are disqualifiers. We look for disqualifiers that say their attitude might not fit within our core values. This is the core of Reverse Hiring™.

Our Attitude Red Flags

- Does the candidate culturally line up with your mission and values?
- Does the candidate seem like somebody who immediately thinks that someone else is at fault? In our environment, you can't be a finger pointer for problems.
- Is the person someone who looks externally for answers to problems, or do they look internally? If you're looking outside of yourself, then you probably don't have the right attitude to be on the team, and we'll tell you that. It's one of our core values.

Promote Your Best to Management!

Attitude, effort, and ability also matter for managers. However, managers require additional consideration. A classic mistake that a lot of business owners make is to take their most competent person and throw them into a managerial role. The owner thinks, "Well, of course they should manage people! They're best at getting stuff done!" And they're wrong.

The two have no correlation, but it's what we do. We take the most inventive and best-thinking person and say, "You know what? You're great at marketing, so you're probably good at managing marketing people too. Why don't we have you manage people?" In reality, being a good manager requires a very specific skill set.

Attitude: When I was in college, I had very little or no financial support from my family. That's not whining. It's just the reality of my life. In addition to taking out loans, I did all kinds of odd jobs. One of those odd jobs was at a restaurant. I quickly moved from a server's role to the front of the house manager. It was a dual-role I had in a few different places during my tenure.

Why was I always put in this role? I had the right attitude. If a table needed clearing and it wasn't in my section, I wouldn't look around to see whose job it was, I would just do it. If the dishwasher called off sick, guess who was washing dishes? If we needed to clean the bathrooms and everyone was busy, well guess what? "That's not my job" was not in my vocabulary.

Effort: If there's one place where effort is needed the most, it's in a manager's role. You may have noticed that I was willing to do everything no matter what my official title was at a restaurant. I was willing to work hard. Everyone, including the managers, had to be able to serve at the lowest level and be willing to put in the effort.

When you are a manager, your job is about serving the team to make sure that they get their jobs done correctly. And you are the person entrusted to remove barriers holding the team back from peak performance. One of my dearest friends says in his organization: "If service is beneath you, then leadership will always be above you." If you're not willing to serve at the lowest levels of your business, then you're always going to answer to somebody. Or worse yet, you got a manager's role and the company is suffering because you're in the wrong place.

Ability: A manager's key ability is flexibility. Think of politics: Someone who is extremely right wing is stuck to their beliefs. They're not willing to change them. Someone who's very left wing has the same exact ideology, just on the opposite side of the spectrum.

Someone who is more moderate might move as long as it stays within certain principles. That's how managers are to us: they have to be capable of good organization and detail but understand that the dishwasher might call off or you might not hit a deadline. That's what we do to change and pivot in an organization. We look for someone with the ability to become a little quicker on his or her feet.

At Fully Accountable™ we constantly have to flex and bend with the situation. One thing we know is that there is always a mess to clean up!

Jim Jensen was an amazing, gifted athlete who played tight end for the Miami Dolphins when I was growing up.[14] He probably wasn't the best tight end in the NFL, but he was a great athlete. He was so good that he could probably be the second best punter on the team. He could easily have been the second or third string quarterback. He could have been fourth on depth chart for wide receivers. He was able and agile enough to maintain multiple positions. As a matter of fact, Jim Jenson did just that for the Miami Dolphins in his career. It's that kind of flexibility that we look for in a manager.

Types of Managers

Quarterbacks

A quarterback is someone left in charge of the organization. They are the fully developed form of a manager. They start with projects, like getting a new campaign or product live. Through their work, this person gathers the skill set to grow into managing a division, an organization, or even a company.

"Entre-leaders"

Entrepreneurs are not the best team players, and that's why we need to make sure we don't duplicate ourselves. However, that doesn't mean we shouldn't bring other entrepreneurial people on our team. We should instead shop for "entre-leaders," people who think like an entrepreneur in their course of the business.

Dave Ramsey (the financial author and motivational

speaker) coined the term "entre-leader" to describe the need for entrepreneurial spirit within his team.[15]

Dave's managers and leaders have entrepreneurial spirits. It doesn't mean that they want to go off on their own, but they have traits and characteristics of entrepreneurs. Dave's core value was: "Be on a team doing it, not alone." I love this. Entrepreneurial spirits who prefer to work on teams do exist. Most people do want collaboration.

Hidden Gems

One of the best guys I've ever worked with is Jeff, a business partner at one of our companies. He interviewed horribly, telling me very specifically what he was and wasn't going to do. Thankfully, we were able to see through his poor interpersonal skills. Then, when he got the job, he turned to be one of the best, most hard-working people on our team.He understood our customer-centric mission so well that he quickly rose to become a partner in our hosting company. Now Jeff is a core partner with four of us in the small SEO firm that we own together. He's killing it.

Each part of our company has a process and a system. I know what our core values and our mission are, and I hold to certain standards by hiring for effort, attitude, and ability. Rather than relying on the person's ability to interview well, I ask myself all of the crucial questions about the candidate and the job we are trying to fill. "Maybe this person is saying some weird stuff, but do they seem to agree with our mission? Are they hard working? Do they have the right attitude? How did they score against our core values?" Thanks to our system, I was able to look past some really bad answers and see potential in Jeff.

Trojan Horses

Unfortunately, I have plenty of lessons in the other direction too. There have been people who've interviewed very well, and then I later found myself wondering whether they switched into a different body once they start working.

Yes,there are some outliers who interview really well and then something tragic happens in their life and they change, but for the most part if someone joins your team and acts different, you were blinded during your interview process. There was something you liked so much that you ignored the warning signs. It's almost always the interviewer's fault.

When someone interviews well, there's usually something about them we like, so we ignore the other signs. To avoid this, interviews should be structured to get to the core of who people are. This should not be a guessing process.

The key to filtering Trojan Horses out of the interview process is to start asking questions that don't have right or wrong answers. Ask questions that are more philosophically based on their personality. And your questions should be gauged to filter through your core values. You will quickly find out if their answers are inconsistent because they are going to give the answers you want, not the ones they actually believe.

You're Hired

99% of companies hire whoever is the "best." Every one of us hunts for the best, and guess what? I don't even think that we understand what that means! So many companies have the hiring process backwards — they shop for competence first because they think it's more important than any other aspect.

I know that the best hire for our company is someone who understands our mission and lines up with all of our core values. When we interview someone to join our team, we're looking for ability, effort, and attitude. They need to come to me with the right attitude, the right ability, and the right effort to learn to execute with the rest of my team. This is why hiring the right people is such a crucial facet of the owner's mindset. And, even more importantly, why it's so essential to determine the company mission, values, and culture prior to hiring; and why you must look beyond ability, and into attitude, effort, and personality, when placing someone new in your organization.

Conclusion

Companies that are going to grow to the next level must have a great team. You do not have to hunt for the "unicorn" for this to happen in your company. Follow these proven steps of hiring and training and you will be well on your way to assembling and growing a world-class team.

Earlier in the chapter we discussed the perfect interview. Go to www.thetotalceo.com/mindset for access.[16]

Also this conclusion is brief but please do not take this as a reflection on the importance of this chapter. I truly believe that the proper team is the single most important ingredient for good and great companies.

Chapter 3

Your Real Numbers

"Show me a company that scaled and I will show you that the same company knows it's real numbers." –Vinnie Fisher

In most small businesses, the owner, the owner's spouse, or some nice person in the office acts as the bookkeeper. In other words, accounting and data management systems in most small businesses are woefully unsophisticated. Because of this, companies get themselves in trouble if they aren't careful. Let's take a closer look at some of the critical mistakes small businesses make when it comes to managing their numbers.

Mistake #1: Inaccurate Reporting of the Numbers

When I began starting companies, I was a great salesman who only cared about one metric: gross revenue. I would walk in every day and all I would want to know was the sales numbers from the day before.

In 2008, I owned a digital publishing company. We were doing almost $10 million a month in revenue. At that level, with so much money changing hands, if you don't watch daily activity (we weren't), you won't know if anything bad will happen until it's too late (we didn't).

We woke up one day and realized something was drastically wrong with the numbers. We were growing but we were *losing* cash. Upon closer examination, we discovered we had a $4 million credit card fraud issue. The company had people driving sales over a 90 day-period, and of the $30 million we brought in, almost 15% of it was from fraudulent transactions. It nearly bankrupted the company! We were able to deal with most of the fraud, but the problem had been going on long enough that we had already paid for most of the fraudulent transactions. We had to pay just a little over $5 million back during this time and it crushed our cash flow. This could have been completely avoided had we run daily and weekly reports where someone was actually reviewing the data to observe issues in our company.

It was the first of many lessons in my business life, and it was probably the most influential to me personally. There are certain key metrics in every business that you need to know as the CEO or as the owner. You can have ambition, passion, and great personnel, but if you don't add key metrics, you're going to wake up blindsided.

Mistake #2: Profit Margin

Next, I launched a new company that started to put the lessons I learned into practice. It was a web hosting company and in 2011, we were the fastest growing one on the planet. We were taking in sales like crazy, competing with GoDaddy everyday for the most signups. My focus was on our growth, performance, and little else.

Unbeknownst to us, our healthy growth would soon start killing our company. We had good cash flow because we sufficiently funded our working capital, but we were not watching our margin. We were growing at a 5% loss and it took about six months of massive growth to expose that issue. We put out $30 million in our first year of business before we noticed. Fortunately, we caught it early enough to be able to turn some things around and adjust our direct expenses.

Between 2011 and 2012 we put out just a little north of $50 million in revenue, but the hosting company netted maybe a 3% profit over two years. We looked gigantic but we didn't make any money; the margin in that type of business is typically around 20 to 25%.

The mistake was mine: the owner, visionary, and entrepreneur who was so intent on growing the business that he lacked the foresight to pay attention to the real metrics that mattered. Thankfully, we were able to make money across multiple companies. Otherwise this would be a story about bankruptcy.

The Birth of Fully Accountable™

Before Fully Accountable™, I launched and ran a very large health supplement company.[17] I was grooming one of our quarterbacks to take over that business, and

I had our CFO come into my office every week and hand me these long, convoluted financial statements.

"Hey, when you're done looking at the financials let me know what you see and we can go over it," he would say.

There were two major problems with this. First, I was offended that that the CFO thought I had a magical 30 minutes to just go through the financials each week when I was already trying to run the company. Second, when I did go through them, it just looked like a bunch of numbers. I had no idea which metrics I needed to focus on.

As the owner, if I didn't have them reported to me in a way I could actually look at them, I was taking on another job that I (and most owners and entrepreneurs) lack the expertise for anyway. And because I didn't have the skills to use all the information handed to me, I tended to really push back and truly ignored that part of the business.

One day I had enough. I threw the reports on my desk and asked, "What do you want me to do with that?"

He looked at me in shock and asked, "What do you mean?"

After I told him all of the reasons this system wasn't working for me (rather loudly and in not so kind of words), our CFO left the room. Once I calmed down, we got back together and talked about it.

"You know what would be really cool?" I asked the CFO. "A synthesized report where I can see some information and you can tell me variances in the numbers. Give me the five indicators we care about most on a front sheet, and show me any variances over a 1-day, 7-day, and 30-day period. If it's old enough, I want to see the numbers for this time last year. Don't tell me any conclusions about what to do with our business; I'll make those decisions. Just give me those number variances."

"Great idea," he said. Off he went and came back with what we now call our "interactive management reports." He took our key indicators and put them on a front page. He gave me the answers to our daily, weekly, monthly, and annual report for what those key indicators look like. He highlighted in black and red where they changed and he made comments if the variance was out of the ordinary. This changed everything for us.

The next thing that happened was a big deal. We had all this great software for our business tools, but we weren't watching them because everyone was always busy doing something and our health company couldn't afford a big accounting department. Finally, we told one team member: "Your daily job is to sit on top of this dashboard and spit out the statistics we need to know." We now call these important statistics the Daily Report. We have a financial analyst who crunches the numbers of our business every day. They tell us the top five things that we need to know. They also have to report something on each one. We need to know a good thing, a bad thing, a variance, an up, or a down. We don't care about anything else. (...Well, we do — but we don't need to get it from him.)

That report saved us money right away, and it continues to do so. Here are some examples:

1. We found out we were holding too much inventory.
2. We realized a new product wasn't selling.
3. We knew when our average ticket numbers were down.
4. We found a number that changed 23 days earlier realized that it was because we had launched a new product that was not working.

And the list keeps going.

Since we only focus on numbers coming from someone who actually spends time watching them, we know the status of every metric intimately. That changed the profitability of our business overnight.

We were doing this for ourselves and we excitedly bragged about it to our friends. Their response was, "Hey, do this for us." So we started doing it for one or two friends who got the same results. Those friends started bragging about it to their friends and, one morning, it came to me. I realized we should offer this as a service for small businesses because it would help them get through the cost barrier of staffing such a role while enabling them to focus on the numbers that really matter. I knew it would revolutionize other businesses just as it had mine.

That very day, our CFO and I sat down and dreamed up how we would bring this idea into reality. We knew the most important things small businesses need but can't have due to money or time constraints:

1. A bookkeeper (the person who enters the numbers);

2. A staff accountant (the person who handles the monthly reporting for the company);

3. Data Analyst (the person who reports and analyses the stats); and

4. A CFO (the Chief Financial Officer, who is a part-time executive on the company team).

We realized something about each position:

1. **Bookkeeper**: Today, there are services all over the place that offer entry-level bookkeeping. The key here is to get the proper entry work done not just go with the cheapest service. What we have found with the low-end source is that you, the owner or CEO, end up doing most of the work — or worse, your office person does the entries wrong.

2. **Staff Accountant**: Small businesses need a staff accountant to deal with the actual grind of doing the day-to-day work: finances, expense structures, making sure the reporting is correct etc. It doesn't have to be a full–time position if it's done efficiently.

3. **Data Analyst**: The key to connecting operations with accounting is creating and analyzing daily and weekly reports. This person is dedicated to analyzing the metrics and operational indicators.

4. **CFO**: Most American businesses only need a CFO three or four hours a month. This is the Financial Executive of the Company. He or she helps with the critical decision about the Financial Management of the Company. With Fully Accountable™, you can have "Your Own CFO" ™ on an as needed basis in cost and commitment.

We also figured out a way to bundle those three services into one and offer it to small businesses. We focused on interactive financials, a CFO, and daily stats. This became Fully Accountable™; a back-office solution that provides outsourced accounting services to small businesses. Our lifeblood is daily stats and Your Own CFO™. We ask every business, "Do you know your numbers every day?" If you don't, find someone to do it now. If you can't afford it we ask, "What parts of your salary are you willing to reduce to invest in this so you can become a more profitable and consistent business?" We filled a gigantic hole in the marketplace and in the online digital world we are helping a lot of companies survive and thrive!

Find Your Metrics

The fact of the matter is, all small companies will inevitably encounter financial or cash flow problems—it's not an *if* but a *when*. Having the right systems and business processes in place so your company has reasonable visibility to protect you from these times is critical. This will help you make informed decisions when there's a problem, which is of paramount importance.

Each industry has different key performance indicators (KPIs) that they need to pay attention to each day. Each industry has around seven key metrics, but there are three to five you have to watch like a hawk. **As an owner or entrepreneur, you have to learn what your key metrics are and put them into place. Doing so will put you on the path to avoiding disaster and make your business a more successful company.**

There's no one-size-fits-all solution. If you're in the retail sector, food industry, or digital marketing, you'll need to know the different metrics for your business. I would say products, services, and hospitality businesses have unique metrics, and within those large industries you can have key metrics that differ as well.

At the hosting company I used to own, we had three key metrics:

- The average lifespan of a customer.
- The average ticket amount we needed to come in the door.
- The industry standard on rebill rate for customers.

If we didn't watch those numbers and manage the business to those key metrics, we would be dead. Fully Accountable™, on the other hand, is a service business. We have completely different key metrics. Listed below are the three metrics we value most:

1) Use of Your Professionals

Like with every service business, whether it's a law firm, an accounting firm, or a consulting practice, the first key metric is the utilization of your professionals. How much are they being utilized compared to the revenue of your business? If you don't know the utilization rate of your service professionals, then you won't know how much to charge. It's the first metric to watch so we know if we're charging correctly. We use this a lot with advertising agencies who have a service component to their business.

2) Collection Rates

The second thing that's critical in a service business is the collection rate. What are your receivables to payables? If you're a service business that lags in collections, how long does it take you to collect? The amount of time it takes versus the amount of time you need to pay for expenses will directly impact your cash flow's ability to grow your company.

3) Cost of Acquisition

How many services do you need to perform before you charge a client? How much time do you put into it? That's the cost of acquisition, and it's a real number. It's different depending on the type of business, but it's critical. If you're spending $100 to acquire a $50 customer, how long will it be until you break even on that $50?

You must know these numbers and how long you can manage negative cash flow or you are captaining a sinking ship.

Metrics Every Business Owner Should Know

I used to say, "Gross revenue can solve most problems, and as long as you get more revenue you can solve most problems." Focusing solely on gross revenue, however, is very dangerous and almost reckless. If want your business to succeed, you should pay attention to these six metrics:

1) Revenue. Know your sales on a monthly, quarterly, and year-to-date basis. Compare them to your business plan to see if you're behind or ahead.

2) Working Capital = *Current Liabilities – Current Assets*

The capital you have available to work with today. As a rule of thumb, you should have $1.50 to $2 of current assets for every $1 of current liabilities.

3) Gross Profit = Revenue – Direct Production Costs

Your gross profit margin is your sales numbers after cutting the direct costs of getting those sales. In most cases, there should be 50% or more of your sales volume leftover after you subtract your direct costs (cost of goods sold).

4) Profit Margin = (Gross Profit – General and Administrative Expenses) / Sales

If your profit margin is negative, you are losing money. Make sure the number is as good as or better than your industry standard. If the typical profit margin in your industry is 12% and yours is 5%, you're not managing your business as well as your competitors. Find out what you need to do to improve that margin. Believe it or not, this is a more important metric than net profit. It tells you the profit potential of your business and its current products or services.

5) Fulfillment Costs and Inventory

In any product business a key metric is fulfillment costs and inventory. What is the holding time of your inventory versus your turnover rate?

- **In the food industry**, the standard industry average is between 26 and 29% on food costs. If you're above that your food costs will kill your business.

- **If you're in a retail space,** your square foot to revenue number is critical. If you don't know what the square foot costs of your rent are in relation to your ability to bring in revenue and break even, then you won't have the ability to grow your business.

6) General and Administrative Expenses.

There are typically three biggies over which the business owner has a great deal of control. Know these numbers and be prepared to adjust them to the current business environment. They include:

- **Compensation.** This is often one of the largest expenses for any business. When business slows down, you need to be positioned to reduce compensation quickly and decisively. This isn't always fun, but it's a decision that a business owner who knows the numbers must make.

  For almost every business, payroll is always the largest expense. There are exceptions, of course — in some businesses it's your inventory or your food cost — but in most cases, the number that owners look to quickly cut is payroll. Be careful, however. You might cut the wrong people who could continue to help you grow your business, and you could have avoided it had you been watching your key metrics.

- **Marketing.** The largest marketing expense is often advertising. You should be able to turn up or slow down your sales by adjusting your advertising expenditures. If there does not appear to be a correlation between advertising and sales, then there may be something wrong with your advertising strategy. The important point is that if you do not compare your advertising expenses and sales, how will you know the effectiveness of your advertising?

- **Research and development.** R&D effectiveness is not as easy to quantify as advertising. However, the savvy manager sets a budget based on anticipated costs necessary to achieve a certain goal. Be certain to periodically measure your progress by comparing the amount spent with the prox-

imity to the goal. Like compensation and marketing, this is a variable number that must be monitored
and adjusted quickly to meet current needs.

Profit and Loss Statement & Balance Sheet

The profit and loss statement tells you the most important story how your business is performing. This is
where the results of your company's efforts and successes are most often expressed. As a result, many
small-business owners will only pay attention to the
profit and loss statement. They won't focus as intently
on their balance sheet and the story it's telling.

That's a big mistake! You should be intimately aware of
the details of your balance sheet, which affect your business's ability to execute on its business and growth
plans. Drivers in this equation include items in your
company's operating cash cycle (such as investments in
inventory, accounts receivable, and other assets) offset
by the amount of terms extended on payables. You
should also understand how much every new dollar in
sales requires in investment in additional working capital.

Ask and Learn

How can you figure out what your key metrics are in
your specific business and industry?

Research: My kids often ask me obscure questions
and are amazed when I know the answers. "How do

you know that?" they ask. The answer: technology! Information is easily available today and highly accessible. We all have the ability at our fingertips to find out anything we want to know.

Within five minutes, I can find an article on an industry's key metrics (and so can you). I can do a little bit of research, expand on that, and confirm what I need to know.

Ask Around: You could interview some people in the business and talk to competitors. They can share some intimacy on the parts of those metrics that matter to them. For example, if you're in the restaurant business and your food costs 41 percent, speaking to someone who's a restaurateur can give you tips on how to get those numbers down without destroying the product. You don't have to do it, but it's wonderful if you can.

Stories like mine are the reason I think people should have a mentor. Seek out advice from experts, owners, and people who have lived the business life. Don't go at it alone. I built my businesses mentor-less and I learned most of these things through the School of Hard Knocks. The cost of my business education is in the millions, and that's why I want people to learn from me. These stories of why you should know your numbers are tragic. But they are also clearly actionable.

Key Performance Indicators

Every business has a series of key performance indicators (KPIs). Unlike metrics, a KPI is a performance measurement tool that is specifically important to your business and your goals. Certain metrics, like gross profit, are important to every business, but the KPIs you track may be totally different than those tracked by another business.

You can look at KPIs daily, weekly, monthly, quarterly, annually, or on a project-by-project or division-by-division basis to help you measure and predict the overall health and efficiency of your company's operations. The effective use and interpretation of your KPIs can help you do a number of very critical financial management tasks:

- Define and measure your progress toward your goals.
- Make informed budgeting and resource allocation decisions.
- Avoid being blindsided or surprised by weak results.
- Detect fraud, waste, or severe inefficiencies.
- Know enough and make decisions that let you sleep at night and to face your lenders or investors with confidence.
- The net margin of your business measured against your competitive industry.

Remember that as your business grows, you may one day need to raise capital via equity or debt. Lenders will want to see your financial reports. The sooner you're capable of producing (and understanding) these reports, the more secure your foundation for growth. Here are some of the most common key performance indicators used to monitor the financial health of a business:

Sales

Accurate sales figures are the first indicator of business trends. Whether they're increasing, decreasing, or flat-lining, they provide a clear indication of where your business is heading. However, they must be monitored in conjunction with bottom-line performance. Many small-business owners become too top-line focused, and take false comfort in knowing that sales are growing even though margins may be shrinking.

Cash Flow Forecast = (Cash in Bank + Cash Coming In Over Next 4 Weeks) – Cash Going Out Over Next 4 Weeks

You should calculate your cash flow forecast on a week-ly or monthly basis; more often is better, especially during a growth spurt. This number will reveal any cash shortfalls over the next four weeks and your ability to pay your bills at the end of the month.

Debtor Days Outstanding = (Accounts Receivable) 365

This is the average number of days it takes for your customers to pay your invoices. A decrease is a positive sign, while an increase is an issue, as it will affect your cash flow and your ability to keep your creditors current.

Creditor Days Outstanding = (Accounts Payable)365

This is the average number of days it takes you to pay your suppliers. This figure needs to be monitored in conjunction with your debtor days. Ideally the number of creditor days will be equal to or higher than your debtor days. If it's lower, you need to improve your debt collection, reduce your customer's credit terms, or negotiate better payment terms with your suppliers to avoid cash flow problems. This is one of the critical disconnects that can cripple a small company.

Inventory Days or Stock Turnover = (Inventory and Purchases)365

This is the average number of days the inventory you produce or purchase remains in your warehouse or on your shelves before you sell it. The lower the number, the better for your cash flow, which ultimately allows you to grow your business and expand your customer base without straining your resources.

Inventory that's "collecting dust" is costing you money without a return and may be stale, obsolete, or ordered in excess of demand. You need to carefully monitor what's moving and what's sitting and, most importantly, understand why. Stay close to your customers and meet often with your sales team to analyze and discuss any inventory that's stuck on your shelves.

Gross Profit Margin as a Percentage of Sales.

The percentage indicates the price you charge your customers against the prices your suppliers charge you. An increase is generally a very good key indicator, but a break even number or a decrease should alert you that there are flaws in your business model or that overhead is too high or prices are too low.

Profit Before Income Tax as a Percentage of Sales.

Ideally this figure should increase, though a flat line may be acceptable for a period. A decrease, on the other hand, may be a warning sign of further potential losses.

Once you decide on the critical three to five numbers that will determine the success or failure of your business, begin to review and digest them on a daily basis, just as you do your morning coffee or vitamin regimen. These numbers can also form the basis for employee-level rewards and bonuses to help you drive business growth and the achievement of your business goals.

Dashboard and Snapshot Reports

No matter what your business industry, you need to know your critical numbers, and then build a snapshot or daily report to monitor them carefully and compare them to key industry ratios. For example, let's say you own a restaurant. If your food costs as a percentage of sales are 41% and the industry average for a restaurant of your type and size is 28%, that's a red flag that something is very, very wrong. Your dashboard or scorecard will provide these yellow or even red warning lights that tell you when proactive remedial action is needed.

The size and complexity of your business will usually dictate the types of business intelligence systems you'll need, but a process and a reasonable system for analyzing information is necessary even for a smaller, less complex enterprise. Have you ever heard the old saying, "We manage what we measure"? Even owners of small businesses need to act "CFO-like" when it comes to developing internal financial reports and dashboards.

DIY Metrics- Quick Exercise to Figure Out KPIs

If you want to put a system in place by yourself, I would recommend you follow these three steps:

1. Figure out which key metrics are important for your business.

2. Find a way to look at your key performance indicators. This can be as simple as an excel file or as complex as a dashboard software.

3. Hire somebody who can dedicate their day to monitoring and reporting on key metrics. This is the most important part.

Share Your Findings

These numbers should be shared, depending on your culture and leadership style, with others in the company who must also manage to them and should be the basis for daily huddles, brainstorming and longer-term strategic planning.

Get into the habit of producing reports. They should go to the following people:

- Yourself
- Your board of directors, advisory board, and the key leaders of your team with whom you're comfortable sharing financial information
- A coach, mentor or consultant with whom you can discuss your key numbers with candor and confidentiality (optional)

Watch Your Numbers

I've had the privilege of losing more money than most people ever make in their lifetime, and I am confident that this life lesson is going to teach a lot of people something about how to track their numbers. The most important thing is to first identify the key metrics. Every business industry has them. Whether or not they hire a service, every company has a need for some form of an accounting function. Even a talented accountant typically lacks the resources to put together some daily statistics or critical indicators reports. So you're either: (1) not going to track your critical indicators, (2) going to help them do it; or (3) go find a resource like Fully Accountable™ to do it. But until now the third option has generally not been available to small businesses because of the cost and firms not wanting to focus on providing this third party service.

I tell people, "If you're not going to do this then you may be an OK company, but you're never going to be a good or a great company, and you're probably one disaster away from choking yourself to death. The good companies, and the great companies, track their metrics."

Once you identify your key metrics, watch them like a hawk because that's the only way you'll quickly stem a massive bleed. That's where my journey started. Learn my lesson or you may have to start over.

Conclusion

There are two key pieces of any company that wants to not only survive but also thrive. One of them is having a great team, and the other is knowing your numbers. If you cannot know the real numbers of your business, you will literally be stuck and unable to grow to the next level.

To see more about sample metrics you need for your industry go to www.fullyaccountable.com/resources. You will also see those resources on www.thetotalceo. com/mindset .[18]

Chapter 4

Products and Services

"How can you hit a bulls eye if you can't even see the target." –Vinnie Fisher

When Fully Accountable™ first started, we were buzzing with ideas. *Let's go build a fancy dashboard! Let's get real-time analytics! Let's create software with interactive financials! Why should we wait until the end of the month or next quarter to launch all of these ideas?* We had all these dreams, and felt confident our ideas were very valid to our target customer base.

I then had to do something as a leader that was not fun. "Guys, what's our core simple offering?" I asked my team. "If we can't get our focus around the simple offering of our business and start there, we're dead."

In the end, I shelved all of our add-on dreams and forced everyone to consider only the essential basics of our idea. For us, our simple offerings were CFO outsourcing, full back office accounting, daily statistics and accurate reporting. We set aside our exciting ideas and focused on what was executable.

Within a month, we learned the importance of the trust and advice of Your Own CFO™ services. It wasn't even going to be our initial core offering, but we found out smaller businesses wanted a CFO but couldn't afford one. We were able to come up with a product where a business could have Your Own CFO™ for a few hours a month without hiring someone. We would have never known that if we hadn't gotten our core offering out and working. We would have waited until we developed all of those other things.

A year later, we're now launching this fancy mobile dashboard analytics tools that I think our consumers are going to love. I think it's going to increase our business and add some substantial growth to it. If we tried to build a software tool before launching our company, the community could not have helped us mature our offerings. And better yet let us know the importance of the software we launched.

I have burned plenty of businesses. I've had epic failures that happened because I didn't think in this way, and I've got wonderful successes where I did. Fully Accountable™ could have gone wrong during that very first meeting, but it didn't because I knew how to execute a service as a leader.

The Problem with Product or Service Development

It's crucial for the leader to have the right mindset on these issues. Almost every business failure can come back to the leadership because ultimately, if you have bad people on the team, whose fault is it? If you have poor execution, whose fault is that? There is one main culprit for failed products and services, and it all comes down to the leader focusing too much on strategy over-development and not getting the best minimally viable product out in the marketplace.

Overdevelopment

I remember one energy bar company that came into our education center. They laid out this whole line of products they had developed. The concept behind their line was amazing, and they had, I'm not kidding you, 45 or 50 products.

The founder sat across from me and said, "You know, we're going to be this big brand."

I said, "Cool, are you there now?"

He gestured to the array of products and replied, "We're going to do all these things—"

"Which product is your number one?" I asked.

"Well, we're still in development," he said. "We're getting them all ready."

I was shocked. "Your company is going to fail," I said. "I'm very sorry for you, but you have a great product that the marketplace is never going to enjoy."

The founder looked at me, alarmed.

I stopped him and said, "You're never going to have a chance to show it off because you're worried about next season. You're going to kill a great product long before this year is over."

He said, "I've never heard this before."

I said, "Be in *this* season. Here's what you need to do. What do you think is your number one product right now? Have you gone out to marathons or given them out to get some people excited about the product?"

"Yes," he said, pointing to one particular bar. "This one is our number one."

"Great!" I said. I swept all the other products out of the way. "Let's focus just on this one. Get this one live right now. You can have a "coming soon" section or whatever you want for all the other ones so that people can see that you have a diverse product line coming, but only focus on this one."

"Why?" the founder asked.

"You had this vision of the whole product line to serve people," I explained. "If you make the whole line live at once, you're going to be playing so far behind that you're never going to catch up. The shame is you're going to run out of money and realize your dream is never going to happen. If you start simply and live on this one bar, you're going to learn a lot of things you don't already know *without undermining your system or burying yourself with overdevelopment.* You stand by this product by itself, make some money, and get ready to launch the rest of your line."

The founder literally hugged me when he got up.

I'll bet you that company is destined for success if he adheres to what I said to him, because he's going to release a great energy bar and he's not going to strap the company with overdevelopment. He's going to get live fast and let his number one product help the marketplace.

Pride of Ownership

When you have been developing something, whether it's ownership of a home, creation of a business, or the growth of a relationship, it is a significant thing in your life. The commitment to see it through regardless of the circumstances is powerful once you get to a certain point a principle of ownership. You've invested so much time that you don't want to stop and give up. Because of that ownership mentality, you're going to be less likely to evolve when it's time to pivot or change.

This happens a lot on the software side of our practice. Our programmers are some of the smartest engineers I've ever worked with, and engineers typically try to build software in a way that encompasses everything. They overbuild. It's not because they are amazing guys who can make a computer dance on its head; it's because they want to build it in a way that they would use it.

This is what I call "Pride of Ownership." It can be a good thing, BUT if it goes too far it can be a real problem. You can get so married to your original vision that you'll lack the ability to change. You can't respond to good criticism. You can't understand what your service or product needs to actually be versus what you *want* it to be. Pride of ownership can kill product development.

So how do you avoid getting stuck in overdevelopment or developing an obstructive case of Pride of Ownership? The key to fixing this issue is understanding your vision and your unique value proposition.

Vision

Vision is a tricky thing for the entrepreneur. You can't be rigid, but you also want to stay true to the goal of your product. That path can change (it can even diverge a little bit), but it ultimately has to come back to this mission or goal.

Documenting the Vision

When you have an idea for a product, you need to set a path so you know where you're going. You have to put out an initial draft of what the final product can look like — think of it as a destination. If you build in a different direction because other people start manipulating your idea, you'll lose your vision, just as you would never arrive at your destination if you start walking in a different direction. All of a sudden you'll think, "How did we get here?"

It all starts with the mindset of the owner, the CEO, or members of the leadership team, and with a clear (and clearly documented) vision. Once you have that down, the vision will always be your guidepost. If you start having a breakdown in the product, you quickly go back to why you made it in the first place. It will allow you to course-correct as necessary, so you don't end up lost. **After all, how can you know you hit a bulls eye if you can't even see the target?**

Staying Flexible Within the Vision

While it's important to have a clear vision, it's just as important to stay flexible as you move down the path. I think the unfortunate part of having a clearly defined vision of a final product is that it sometimes translates into people believing they have to build *that* final product. I have done this so many times. I come up with a product or service and I have a vision for what I think the final product is, and you know what? When we finally get to some version of a final product, it's different. It's rare (extremely rare) that we're anywhere near that drawing, but the drawing gave us something to measure and build towards.

Staying True to the Vision

If the vision leader doesn't stay on the concept, and instead builds a product in another direction because of demand, that's fine. But remember to be careful. Service businesses have this problem. We start delivering a service and people say, "Well, do you do it this way?" Don't let the culture of someone who has not set the path start dictating the direction you want to go. It's a very dangerous thing to happen to a service or a product.

As leaders, CEOs and owners, we're idea tinkerers. We always want to move on and create something new. When we leave something behind and we're not there to manage its path, that's when the business typically fails. When it shutters, everyone says, "Wow, we didn't have the right CFO in place! We didn't have the right people on the team!"

But those are just indicators. The core reason for the failure rests solely with the owner or CEO. The business lost a clear vision of their products or service. The leader moved away from it. Over time everything else slowly crept in that direction, and ultimately killed the company.

The Team

At Fully Accountable™, our goal is simple: we take the process of knowing your numbers and move it into key indicators for each of the company's operations. By pushing the data through to simple reports, you can operate your small business easily and without guessing; it's something new in the industry and we're all excited about it.

But our chief programmer got it sideways and started building a complex version of the reports, tying them together with all of the accounting practices. It was a great idea for the middle and large companies, but completely out of line with the direction we were going. Small businesses need simple reports and we almost killed the great idea in over-development.

I asked him, "What happened? Why were you doing that?" He responded, "I think we really need this."

"But where did that idea come from in the first place?" I asked him.

After our conversation I realized he had lost the mission, and that it was 100% my fault. As discouraging as it may be, as the CEO, if you don't accept ownership of the loss of mission then you'll never be able to lead your people correctly. They'll get lost. You have to keep them on the path.

Constantly talk about the mission and push back at every development phase to understand why deviations happen. If the team doesn't know where they're going, they're not going to know what to do. **It's also important to continuously reinforce the mission and the vision.** If they don't have a clear vision, they won't do anything.

This is exactly what happens in product and service development. The leader gets extremely frustrated because the team is not focusing on the original vision. The team gets frustrated because they're not sure where to go or what to do. That's why a clear vision has to not only be set, but also continually followed and reminded.

New People

I was in a meeting with one of our newest project managers. He sat down with me and laid out a social media strategy for one of our brands. I looked at it and said, "I need to apologize. I think you just wasted about 20 hours of work." He looked a little alarmed.

"What is the core mission of this company?" I asked him.

He looked at me. "To increase revenue and get customers," he said.

That explained everything. "This is all on me," I sighed, "I did not do a good job of explaining our vision to you."

I spent the next half hour explaining the core vision of the company and what we do. I'll bet I told him during his interview and in our weekly meetings, but it never sunk in; or maybe it went away over time because he didn't *own* it and I wasn't there to reinforce it. He never became a disciple of the mission.

Finally, he got up and shook his head.

"I would have done this entirely differently had I known that," he said.

This happens so often it's not even funny. Defining the clear path constantly is something leaders don't know they signed up for, but they did. I learned over time that the leader of an organization has to be the closest to the new people.

There's a word and sentence that should never be spoken by any leader in any company: "Who's the new person?" A small business has less than ten employees, but leaders still ask that question all the time. It's scary to me because a new employee is going to get a diluted version of the mission and value of the company. If a boat leaves London for New York, but it's one degree off on its coordinates — instead of landing in New York, it and ends up in Nova Scotia. It's the same thing with our new people. When they get a diluted version of the mission and value, they head in the wrong direction. This is why it's essential for the CEO to stay close to them, especially in their first few months.

Move Fast and Break Things

Until 2014, Facebook's motto was "Move fast and break things." [19] We love that motto at Fully Accountable™. Get something up fast — the first version of your product or service doesn't have to be perfect. If you focus on the key deliverables and make that work, you can work on the rest of it with time.

I believe in getting the earliest version of a product out quickly, provided that it's good and meets the promises of expectations. Your consumers and community can provide you with the proper feedback to make sure you're on the right track. It also allows you to work in a live environment while making your product better for the people that are actually going to use it.

Just Do It

So many people have spent so many hours developing a product or a service to the point of overdevelopment — so much so that the principle of perfection sets in. You can never get the product out because it's not "ready"; it's not developed enough. I've seen so many people, not only in our own businesses, but also those we've acquired to the team or those I've mentored whom literally cannot complete a product. It is one of the most fatal underlying errors that pervade the thought processes of many leaders throughout the world.

Get rid of the assumption that a product has to be completely developed before you launch it to the world and get value. What happens with most CEOs is that we start anticipating breakage, adaptation, and a need for pivoting. This leads to the excuses that you hear constantly: "the launch is delayed," or, "we'll roll that out when it's really ready." That's just a form of execution paralysis. When we do that, we rob our company of the ability to get stuff out and improve them as we go—and we rob the community of a great product.

Something can be good without being perfect. I grew up relatively poor by today's standards. My grandmother used to say to me, "Being poor doesn't mean you have to be dirty." She had a very well kept home and everything was clean. If you looked in from the outside, you'd think everything was great because of my grandmother's efforts in keeping her home clean and organized. It looked very nice at all times. You can look and act a certain way without being perfect — and we were the embodiment of that rule. That was a big lesson in my life that I apply to my products. So your products and services can be very good at any stage of its development, even if all features or offerings are not completely available.

Worry About This Season

It's easy to worry about the next season of our life and business. We're planning for what's ahead, which has some value in it but all too often takes us away from our current season of life. You've got to build a projection and have goals, of course, but it's essential to your business that you're able to live within the season we're in *now*. You will stay more focused and stay on path. Your productivity will definitely increase.

I've given the exact same advice to clients in a firm that specialized in the optimization of marketing channels, and they had so many opportunities to do so many things.

"What's your core offering?" I asked.

"We can get a sales channel live faster and in a very effective and simple way."

I said, "Great! Start there."

They did that for 18 months. They started by offering simple streamlined channels live, faster than everyone else. That message and motto got out fast. They've grown so much in that one delivery of their service that they're unable to add anything else to their service right now; but they have a valuable business that stuck to a very simple "get it live, worry about this season" mentality. I am looking forward to the start of the next season of their business — but only when they are ready for it.

Make Something New

Here's how I see it: if you're not constantly making something new, you're standing still; and if you're standing still, your business is probably dying.

It's a strong statement, I know. All businesses, not just new startups, should be making new stuff. That doesn't necessarily mean a new service; it could be a new way you're offering the same service. It could mean changing up the delivery schedule. It could be a change in the way you communicate with the end user. It could simply be improving or enhancing your existing product.

But there is a struggle that must be addressed here. Yes, a business must continue to improve and add new elements, offerings, products and services. But too often, the business does this too quickly and is scattered. **Wait too long and you are stale. Move too fast and you're over-extending.** So, yes this is tricky. I recommended earlier that the way we handle this issue is to always be "developing" and "adding." But do not disrupt your current team in order to do so.

Relinquish Ownership

I always have to remind our programmers, "You're not building software for yourself. You're building it for an end user. What is it that *they* want?" It's important to understand that the service you deliver or the product you have belongs to the customer, not you. Once you realize that the customer is actually who you're building it for, you'll start building better products that are better suited to the people you are servicing.

As an inventor or creator, the idea person, you are doing something of value; but in the end it's the users, not the creators, who have the most control. It's a very interesting struggle. When you can understand this psychology right away as an owner, creator, or even as a leader within someone else's organization, it's powerful.

Technology and Product Development

Technology has made it so much easier to bring your product or service into the marketplace. Just think about writing as an example. In order to be a writer even just a couple decades ago, you would have had access to a publisher. Self-publishing used to be hard, but now getting a book live is easy and that has leveled the playing field for any writer to get into a marketplace.

The same exact thing is true for products and services for businesses. You do not need to have a large development team. You don't need to have designers and developers. You don't have to have a large budget. You can build something that meets all your specifications, refine your marketing message, and improve it as you go.

You can look at a product that is already on the shelves and refine it to meet your standards. In fact, I recommend doing so if you are a business that does not have a lot of capital. It will move quickly and put your effort into two critical areas:

- Messaging to your customer.
- All the parts of the system necessary to the supply chain, delivery, and the execution of your product or service.

Why are these the most important? The consumer has already decided that they want a certain product. It has been made before. It may not be an uninhibited marketplace, but you also didn't blow everything trying to build to a great product that no one is ever going to see. I can go pick a product off the shelf or duplicate a service because technology has allowed me to watch what competitors do.

In the product business there are demand-type systems that allow for the production of the building, manufacturing, and delivery of a product not even on your own campus. I used to own a health supplement company, but the company didn't own a fulfillment house. It didn't have any inventory sitting on the floor of that business. All of that was done via an on-demand relationship with the fulfillment manufacturer. As a business grows we can take on some of that development internally to save costs, but thanks to technology we don't have to until we're ready.

What it comes down to is this: the message that "you have to do it all" is hurting many good companies. The shame is a lot of good products (and a lot of very smart people) fail in a business because they've had to burn all their money on product development. The actual product then never gets out to the marketplace because they ran out of cash.

The best way to avoid the pitfalls of "you have to do it all" is to collaborate, use available technology, and outsource relationships. Can you get to the market quickly? Then move fast. Use today's technology to move into a marketplace faster than you ever could have before.

Consistent Execution

I think everyone should work in a retail service business — there is no better way to learn how to deal with people. I put myself through college and law school while working in the hospitality business, mostly in restaurants and bars. I learned when you wait tables the diner won't know whether you're giving them good or bad service unless they've been served by you or someone else before; whereas if you deliver poor service to a regular who is used to excellent service, they will catch it right away.

Once you deliver a certain standard of service and have a repeat customer, you must give them that exact same standard again if you want to meet their expectations. If you don't, they'll be disappointed. It won't be because they measured you against some other service standard, but because you gave them a standard with which to measure you.

Let's say a customer calls our customer service line and we tell them to wait five minutes. Right away, that's always going to be our standard because if they do wait five minutes then they'll always expect that. But if you tell them they're going to wait 30 seconds and they instead wait five minutes, the consumer is going to be extremely upset.

I tell our team that we need to deliver for the expectation we set the first time we serviced a client, not a standard to which we might not be able to meet. We have to provide services with the same consistency. If you don't, you're going to lose the trust of your client base.

I don't believe that having the best product always wins over customers. What really matters is consistently meeting the expectations of the end user. I think we have to strive for a great product, but having the best one should not be our goal. That's the scary thing: you can't strive for both progress and perfection. True perfection is unattainable.

You need someone on your team to advocate for consistency. As the leader, you may not be able to do it all the time. I've found over time that it is essential to have a person dedicated to service consistency in the organization. We have one at Fully Accountable™ whom we actually call our "consumer experience person." This person secretly shops at our business every day. Why do we do that? We want to be consistent on our expectations of delivery. It's amazing how consistency of expectation can change the entire relationship with our customers. It's what makes it so critical.

Passion Ambassadors

Passion ambassadors are the key customers of your business. They love you because you have delivered consistent product execution and you have over-delivered on your customer's expectations. If you do those things, people will brag about your product or service regardless of whether you ask them. That's a critical standard in product development. If you can have 100 passion ambassadors, your business is destined for success. At Fully Accountable™, our mission is *"to help small business owners know and understand the numbers, gain control of the business, free up the money and resources to scale, and get back the time to invest in their mission."*

We have a gentleman in the Midwest who has a wonderful lifestyle health company. He's a big Crossfit guy, but he has also formulated some excellent supplements and built a great a community. The problem was that he was focused on ambition and growth, and not on managing his key metrics and indicators. His company was doing about $3 million gross revenue a month, and they were losing money. Remember: *It's not about gross revenue; it's about what you keep that determines continued success.*

As soon as we started watching their key performance indicators, we eliminated four accounting positions for his company! The CEO had thought that hiring more and more staff — office accountants in this case — was a way to solve the problem because he didn't have the time or expertise to deal with knowing the numbers. We came in and became their CFO, their staff accountant, data analyst and their bookkeeper for less than what he was paying the lowest-paid accountant on the team.

We started doing their daily statistics and very quickly jumped on the problem areas. This business had major issues in its margin and in customer acquisition. We went in and helped him eliminate the five or six obvious expense nightmares in the business. He quickly cut his fulfillment cost from 18% to 12%, cut four or five major staff positions that meant nothing to the success of their business, and he cut five or six traffic targets.

The first month we came in and stopped the bleeding, his $1.5 million in gross monthly revenue resulted in a 10% margin – they made $150,000. The next month we got them to a little over $200,000 in profit. Today, they're averaging a million dollars and operating at about 23% profit margin.

Needless to say, this guy loves us to death. He tells everyone about us, and he isn't the only one. We've got dozens of people who are passion ambassadors for us. We helped them realize the importance of focusing on their key metrics so they could make good business decisions, and in return, they spread the word about the value of our business. Building Passion Ambassadors happen when you deliver a good product consistently.

Conclusion

The visionary/creator sets a clear path, the team gets a product in the marketplace, and the consumer starts providing feedback. This is the cure for overdevelopment. This is how you execute a product or service. Once you start letting your ability to produce eliminate the vision of the perfect product in your mind, you are well on your way to developing an "Execution Attitude" in your product or services department.

To learn more about products and services and how to truly stay on your unique value proposition go to www. thetotalceo.com/mindset and check out the "Execution Attitude" section.[20]

Sales & Marketing

*"Simplicity and focus are the champions
to a winning sales message." -Vinnie Fisher*

The most successful businesses today have one thing in common: a direct sales message offering a product or service that has a clear value proposition to the consumer. As I stated multiple times throughout this book, most company owners have a strong connection to the marketing message or ability to sell the product or service. Or at least we think we do!

Remarkably, as owners and CEOs, we also struggle with ways to develop new tricks, hacks, methods, funnels, or ideas to acquire more customers. When in reality if we spend our time clarifying our offer and positioning our product or service to deliver the value necessary to the end user then we will really see movement in our offering.

I hear from so many clients, friends, and fellow colleagues in the business that all he or she needs is more customers. And to solve that problem, they just need more traffic! So they set out to find new ways to get traffic to the offering the company has put out there. When I get the chance to look under the hood, it's never a traffic issue. The problem is an unclear message or that the proposition or product lacks value.

My dear friend Ryan Deiss spells it out perfectly: "You do not have a traffic problem, you have an offer problem."[21] If you do not know Ryan or are not familiar with him, check out his stuff. He is an excellent marketer who knows how to keep a message simple, direct and focused on value to the consumer.

His words couldn't be more accurate either. As the chief marketer for your group, if you have a "traffic problem" the answer is not another clever sales channel. The answer always lies with your offer and the underlying value proposed. Stop and focus on the clarity and simplicity of your offer. Does your offer convey the value of your product or service?

I guarantee that if you fix this issue, you will NOT ever have a traffic problem. In other words, stay focused on providing more value instead of more marketing efforts.

Customers Come First

The biggest issue I have with strategy as it is today is it has changed from, "What do we want to deliver to the consumer, and how are we going to accomplish that?" into, "What's the best idea I can come up with? What's the new hack, the new tool that's going to set *me* apart?" The second approach doesn't consider what the consumer wants. It has changed from "How can I deliver value?" to "How can I get ahead?" Now let me ask you: which approach do you think yields better results?

That's my big picture issue with strategic planning. In sales and marketing, it's about delivering a value proposition message to the consumer. Wanting more sales is not a bad thing — but in most cases it's where things start to run amok. Owners get caught up trying to figure out their share in the market, their competitive landscape, and whom they are when quite honestly they need to stop and focus for just a few minutes and ask themselves, "What is it we really want to offer someone? What is our unique value proposition? What is our unique selling proposition? What do we sell or offer that puts us in a different position from our competitors?"

Unique Value Proposition

Have you lost your focus and commitment to delivering a valuable offering to your consumer? The solution to this issue is simple but, unfortunately, it's not easy. You've got to offer products and services to people who see the offering as valuable. This is difficult because it's not the shortest path to sales. It's much harder to offer products that people want to keep coming back to buy from you.

Many companies start out with a decent plan and a mission to offer value. Then with growth and lack of margin or profitability, we quickly rush to making more sales and do not invest in continuing to improve on the value offered to our customers. This continues over time. And after a while our vision and mission, unless clearly stated, is no longer in focus. We now serve the master of more sales and revenue rather than customer loyalty and feedback.

Is your company suffering to break through to its next level? Do you have sales coming in but you cannot seem to maintain stability or consistent growth? Are you jumping from one product to another for more revenue? If you answered yes to any of these questions, I suggest you are struggling with value in your offering. "You don't have a traffic problem, you have an offer problem."

If you want to fix this problem and break through to the next level your company is capable of achieving then you need to get back to the simplicity and focus that got your company started in the first place. Now I am not suggesting that you go back to the first season of your business. I am recommending that you achieve the focus and simplicity of the first season.

Simplicity and Focus

So many times as one of my companies would start to see significant growth, my first reaction was to start adding more products or services. Our list of offers would significantly increase because we wanted to scale quickly. And before long, we would be on dangerous ground because we had a bunch of revenue and sales and a new base of customers that sadly were not going to be around very long.

Now after many mistakes and successes, along with helping many clients achieve the same results, I know that reducing the amount of offers and simplifying the message and focus is the true way to achieve scale that will last.

I recently met with a client that was having problems with the team losing focus and having low morale. Plus the sales of the company were volatile. I asked the client if we could meet as the entire executive team and discuss these issues. During this meeting, I found out from the operations director that the company had over time tripled its number of products and offers.

And worse yet, I found out that only a few offers and a few products accounted for the substantial revenue in the company. I asked the team what would happen if we eliminated all of the other products and offers. As you may suspect, the entire team was first shocked that they would even be allowed to do this but also relieved that such an option would even be possible.

So we decided to eliminate almost 80 percent of the additional products. And almost immediately the company started to experience real growth, a more energized work environment, and overall peace and joy in the workplace. It was all due to the team choosing simplicity and focus. The choice to simplify the product line and the focus to drive sales on the winners and ignore the low performers made all the difference.

We're all guilty of veering away from simplicity in the name of sales. As soon as we experience some success, we want more quickly. And we grow outside our ability and mission in order to chase success. But it's never too late to course-correct and reset your focus.

Mission and Values

If you have lost your way, I suggest you go back to the basics. You can return to your original mission, or stop and develop a written mission that clearly and succinctly defines your company and its vision. This is not a wasted exercise. As we've already discussed, you need to create a clear focal point for your company. And quite honestly, if you do not have a mission then your path is not clearly illuminated. Without a clear path, why would you be surprised then that you are all-over the place?

Exercise: Take a blank piece of paper and write out your mission for the company. Even if you had one originally, write one now and see what it looks like for this season of your company. Sit with your team and work on revising it to a simple one-sentence (two at maximum) message.

After you complete the above exercise, start doing a complete company overview of your actions and priorities. I will guarantee there are many things happening that wouldn't be if you were strictly adhering to your mission. Your next step is to eliminate all of these distractions from the company. This will lead to you getting back on mission and on your way toward breaking through to the next level for your company.

It is the dedication to get back to simplicity and focus that will truly lead your company to success. As I stated earlier, the plan is simple but the execution requires effort. But the effort will pay off with a company positioned to grow to the next level.

Another good reason to complete your mission is to clarify your message to the consumer. Quite often I see many companies suffering with their sales and marketing message because the offering lacks clarity. And usually this is due to a lack of a clear mission.

Clarifying the Message

A company chasing so many ideas, products, and offers usually lacks clarity and focus. Stating your mission will allow you to get a clearer sales message. It's undisputed that a clear sales message will result in more effective sales and better customers.

In order to clarify your message you must: (1) be on mission; (2) remove unnecessary or unproductive sales channels and offers; and (3) have a definite call to action for the customer. A clear result you want to achieve with your sales message.

Once you have defined your mission, you need to work with it for a short while to make sure your team is completely on board, in terms of both internalized understanding and buy-in. (Remember what can happen when they don't.) Once you have decided that the mission is on point then it's time to make sure you have the proper sales channels live for your products.

Proper Sales Channels

Your sales message cannot work in every sales channel. Before we get too far into this subject, I should make sure we are on the same page when it comes to sales channels. There are many sales channels online and offline, but not every channel is going to work for the customers you have or for your products or services. Certain channels are not typical to certain customers. So for example, if you have a recipes offer you are most likely using Pinterest in your sales process. I know this due to the fact that 4 out of every 5 women online have a Pinterest account. You need to go where the customers are and market to them on that channel.

Fully Accountable™ provides back-office accounting solutions for small businesses. We also have a strong expertise in online digital businesses, such as retailers, digital design and marketing agencies and information marketing companies.   We also have a storing base of offline brick and mortar businesses. But not all channels for advertisement of our company would be relevant, and not all of our offers will work the same for each channel. At the date of preparing this book, we have not turned on any paid traffic for our company. It all grows organically!

But here is where our advertising will do very well. Using LinkedIn to acquire leads on companies looking for accounting services.   But our message to online digital companies is different from the message needed for traditional offline businesses. We cannot expect our offers to react the same.

In helping clients clarify their sales message, I usually find out that the same clients are also advertising in either too many or incorrect sales channels. You need to make sure you are running offers in the proper sales channels.

The first thing you need to do is determine the avatar of your ideal customer before advertising in a certain channel. If you don't know what your ideal customer looks like then you should look to the data of your buyers or the data of the buyers in your industry.

Once you have the demographics of your ideal customer, you are then in a good position to determine the places where it would be best to advertise your products to the customer. So for example, if you have a product or service that will appeal to the masses then you should be able to advertise on Facebook and Google. But the offers you present in each of those channels will be different.

While on its face it may seem that the offers in both channels would work the same, Facebook advertising is a display style platform while Google is mostly a search-advertising platform. This may seem very basic to some of you but this difference is critical in how to position the offer for your consumers.

Many clients have gotten so deep into the business that these basic aspects of their marketing plan have been abandoned. So before you start developing a new funnel or sales channel, make sure you are advertising to the right people in the right place. Once you do that, you need to also take into account whether the customer is coming to find you or whether you are looking for them.

I have worked with so many clients that have gone through the process of making sure they are advertising on the right channel and in front of the right customer but still are not seeing many sales. The offer is not competitively converting to allow the client to continue to spend advertising dollars to acquire customers. The reason this client was unable to make the offer competitive was that the call to action was missing or it was wrong.

Call to Action

A good marketer can do all the right work building a good offer for a high quality product. That offer can then be advertised on the right channel to the right customer. And still, the product may fail to gain any sales at a competitive rate due to the offer asking for the wrong action or, worse yet, including no call to action at all.

The key here is to make sure you are asking for the right action. If you have an offer educating a consumer about services that then jumps right to "Buy Now," the call to action may be misplaced or too early in the process.

This actually happened to us at Fully Accountable™. We were having a brief 30-minute call with prospects and having little success. Our break rate on the offer was higher than expected. Our offer was good but we discovered our call to action was too early.

So we decided to change the offer to allow every prospect to come in to do a 30-day review for free. After the review and suggestions, we then made the call to action for our services. After that, our acceptance rate increased, which in turn caused our break rate to significantly drop. If you have a take rate issue, I recommend you review your call to action to see if it is properly placed.

Simplicity and focus, a clear offer, proper positioning and putting the customer first — these need to be the key aspects of the CEO's mindset when it comes to sales and marketing. It can be so tempting to apply our skills toward adding sales, growing traffic, and getting more customers; but when we do, we pull our energy and attention from the areas that will truly enable our company to thrive.

Conclusion

Too many of us entrepreneurs complicate our sales and marketing message. You have a unique sales proposition. Get back to your simple clean message. If you have not developed one go to www.thetotalceo.com/mindset and we have a USP exercise to help you and your team on your sales message.[22]

Chapter 6

Processes and Systems

"Consistent delivery of your product or service is rewarded with brand value and recognition."- Vinnie Fisher

Processes and systems are everywhere. It's the way we get out of bed. It's the way we take a shower, the way we brush our teeth. We rely on the consistency of said processes to get things done in our life and in our businesses. Even the most upfront leader who likes to jump around and be involved in things loves the consistency of following through with a procedure or system. Processes and systems allow you to duplicate success.

> **Process (n):** The way we are trained to do something. If you have a consistent process, then your ability to scale a business should also be consistent.
>
> **System (n):** The overall structure within which each individual business unit works.

Both pieces are essential to the CEO mindset, and in this chapter we're going to see why.

Why You Need Processes and Systems

You have already acquired the wisdom to make good decisions for your business, but is that true for the other members of your team? My guess is no. So if you don't have a system in place, you are leaving your team with little more than guesswork on which to base their decisions — or forcing them to come to you over every little thing.

What would help your employees perform to your expectations? You have to either be willing to personally train them, or give them a business process — something that details a consistent way to offer products or service to your customers. This is a top "aha" moment with my clients. People think, "Holy cow! If I put what I do into a checklist, I can duplicate myself. I free myself up to concentrate on what really matters!" And they're right.

Proper processes and systems do more than free up the owner or CEO's time and energy too. They also provide much-needed consistency.

Consistency

The most respected brand, whether it's a product or service brand, earned its good reputation because of consistent delivery. There's no surprise that the best brands have the most consistent delivery. The reason why Amazon is the fastest growing ecommerce platform is because they have created a consistent expectation of a service that they deliver every time to the consumer.

Apple is another example. Apple has a consistent delivery of a quality product to its consumer. This is not an accident. This is purposeful behavior. Apple won't release a new version of the iPhone with a technical problem because it violates their internal rules. Whether we're talking about iPads or earbuds, a new product doesn't come out until it's perfect, no matter how many people may be clamoring for it.

I had the opportunity to interview Steve Wozniak (co-founder of Apple) back in the day.[23] I saw him at a conference and asked him a question about structures and systems at Apple.

"We followed a structure or system because we knew our vision and our mission and we stuck to that," he told me. "When we were asked to review some new ideas, we knew what filter we were running that through. It helped us make those decisions."

Consistency is our goal at Fully Accountable™; it's one of our core foundational values. A company that's going from a one-person operation to a fully-fledged business has to adapt a mentality of structure and consistency in order to succeed.

The problem is that people think consistency is *boring*. They think they will have to do the same job all the time. In reality, the most significant thinkers, the biggest inventors all the way down to the production workers, thrive on consistency. It's the same thing in any business. A process and system has to be designed on your mission first.

Think about your customer service complaints. They probably always go back to some missed expectation; your company delivered one standard one time and a different standard at another time. In our accounting business, we deliver financials on the 15th. If one month we were to deliver on the 16th without explanation, that alone would change the standard of our commitment to our customers. And there'd better be a reason why that is! It may seem minor, but it would be a breakdown in our system of consistently delivering our product.

The Pilot Analogy

I really liked the book *Checklist Manifesto*.[24] In it the author, Atul Gawande, noted that in the airline industry, processes and systems started with tragedy. There were a few accidents in which lives were lost. In an industry in which mistakes could be the difference between life and death for their customers, they knew they needed a consistent system.

The airline industry asked their best pilots to create checklist outlining how they would start taking off a plane. From there they built out a series of standardized processes. Now, we can rely on commercialization of airlines to follow a consistent standard. Can you imagine a pilot turning to the co-pilot and saying mid-flight, "Jackie, did you remember to check the fuel?" If you have systems and processes in place, you don't run the risk of a critical oversight.

Memory

Standard processes also save energy. If you are a payroll clerk and your worst fear is missing somebody on payroll, the last you want to do is let everybody down. Everyone on the team wants their check on time, with all the deductions taken out correctly. Lots of things have to happen for payroll to be processed, and the payroll clerk wants to do them consistently every time because she doesn't want her team members to be out a paycheck.

The problem is, if the payroll clerk spends a lot of energy trying to avoid a mistake, she might forget something else. Trying to remember the things you *shouldn't* do can cause you to fail. A checklist helps avoid those sorts of problems. As owners and CEOs, we can take the fail rate significantly down by setting our minds on creating a systemized process or checklist for our employees and even ourselves.

My Journey to Systems and Processes

I was not trained to think about systems. My mind does not naturally think this way. Entrepreneurs as a group have never been in the environment of systems, which are more suited to an engineering mindset. It is a learned cultural behavior that starts with the mindset, support and commitment of the leader.

At first, the idea of implementing processes and systems is so overwhelming for entrepreneurs that they won't do it. I've been there. It's like asking, "What part of an elephant do I start biting in order to eat it?" That's what someone who's had to be their own hustler hears when you ask them to add structure or systems or process to their business. And yet, our company is getting better each day at it.

The Leader's Mindset

Before I met Shirley I read a book called *Work the System* by Sam Carpenter.[25] He pointed out that many business owners just rely on memorization and hope that people around us have caught on enough to consistently deliver. I realized that I had been doing just that: doing everything from memory and working really hard to deliver consistency, but not getting any of our team the tools for being consistent. I knew it was hurting my business.

To look at the historical context and say, "Well we didn't do it before we're not going to do it again" is a recipe for failure. So the only agent of change is to wake up and say, "This is something we've not done before but we need this. It's going to require a change in my mindset to pull that off."

Owners need to have the right attitude to be able to scale and grow their business properly. Owners like me set out to change the world and offer value, only to have everything come true and get stuck in a job that they never wanted. They would rather go do something else. Putting the correct systems and processes in place will allow you to do just that. You can then back away and someone else can provide the exact same delivery and consistency in your place.

Implementing systems and processes can feel over-whelming — at least it was for me. I made the mental decision to bring a culture of processes and systems into my business, and immediately felt like I was in over my head. Then I found Shirley, my business consul-tant.

The minute I met Shirley I said, "Listen, I need you to show me how to install these systems into our busi-ness. I have to be the one that implements this idea if my team is going to buy in." I knew the idea wouldn't stick if it seemed like it was coming from an outsider.

She stopped and, I'll never forget this, she said, "Your company is going to succeed at this. You're one of the few who have said to me that you're committed to mak-ing it happen."

I admitted to Shirley that I was nervous, and then I got down to business. "I feel like every team member has a specific job and they are the ones who have to actually document their own job," I said.

Yougetit! Youshouldhavemyjob," Shirley laughed. "Al-right Vinnie, I know this is overwhelming to you, but why don't we break this down and just start in one place? Let's start with your job. Do you have any re-petitive tasks? Stuff that, if we could get it documented, we could bring someone in to do it for you and free up your time?"

At the time, I was in charge of our sales department. I was basically our affiliate manager. The administrative work behind signing purchase orders and generating affiliate links and getting new traffic sources live was very repetitive, so it was the first thing that came to mind. I still wanted to do the sales calls because that was the part I was good at, but I didn't need to do the repetitive work.

I documented how to onboard new affiliate relationships. I basically just wrote down, "Here's the link, here's how you do it, here's how you cement this person, here's what they expect when you deliver over to them." I took the consistent part of what usually produces the best results and built this procedure.

In the end, making a process for affiliate signups was very important to our business. When it was delivered consistently, we had more affiliates. We used that as a basis to build probably the first procedure system I've ever had in our business.

Executing Processes

Shirley helped us take this big concept of implementing systems and processes throughout the entire company and make it very practical, one position at a time. Instead of suddenly telling everyone to start creating processes, we picked a department and a specific person within a department. We started with our big revenue maker, our affiliate department, then we moved into product development, and then we moved into customer service. We went down the line and through each department, getting a system in place, documenting and making checklists for the replicable part of the jobs so that we could deliver consistently to our customers.

It was long and extensive process of breaking down each job into line items, but now we have guides we can use for training and all duties put into a checklist format. These help us make sure everything that needs to get done is completed correctly and on time.

We have since created an electronic system for this process and made it even easier.

Most people have good ideas, but they don't know the steps to take to execute them. But as a company, you need to be continuously experimenting, stopping, and using strategy to support what you've executed. Once you have the right people on your team, you have to fully capitalize on their strengths by training them to execute every single day, until it is as intuitive as breathing for them.

The Scrum Mentality

In my company, we do everything in a scrum environment. Scrum is a style of management that aims for the completion of work. It got its genesis in engineering work, and is commonly used by programmers and other workers of the digital world. It's a way to schedule deadlines so that you're always executing and meeting milestones.

Software people must have an agile environment — a scrum environment — or their products will never meets deadlines or releases. You and I get updates all the time for apps and software. Most of those app developers run on some form of a scrum mentality. So why doesn't every small business have this style of management in the implementation of new ideas and work process?

This is what a scrum mentality looks like at Fully Accountable™: we run a Tuesday to Monday business, and we complete projects on a weekly basis. If something takes a month, then we break it into weekly chunks to manage it. We define and manage the process of how to get through it. We adjust it along the way if we have to, but we are always driving towards a concrete goal.

Every business can work like that, but most businesses don't have the attitude of weekly completion. They probably have a quarterly goal, and it's too big. People have too many opportunities to slide with no direct accountability for days. We learned that pulling our calendar back to a week allows us to break it into 5 working days, and that works perfectly.

We schedule weekly goals within our scrum environment to focus on the highest priorities to be done during the week. We have the right structure in place to work with weeklong attitudes, and we break those attitudes into daily activities. That is the structure of our scrum environment.

To meet our weekly goals, we have to have several meetings per week:

Executive Meeting (Fridays): The executive process team meets every Friday morning to learn our work goals for the Monday meeting. To complete our work every week, there are daily tasks we have to accomplish, and at the Friday meeting we learn which daily tasks need to be prioritized.

Company Meeting (Mondays): We're able to launch the results of the executive meeting on Monday at 4:00 p.m., when the weekly company-wide meeting takes place. There we outline the priority tasks and weekly goals. We need to make sure the assembly line is complete by Monday.

Standup Meeting (daily): Every day the director of our operations has what we call a "standup" at 10:00 a.m., which every employee attends. We stand up as a community and describe one-fifth of the weekly goal we have to accomplish today and why it's important. The next day, we tell the community if we got yesterday's task done and what we're doing today.

The whole meeting lasts less than 15 minutes. Some companies take 30 minutes, but I think that's too long. To keep it short, we let a manager deal directly with anyone who has any breakdowns in their workflow. We call that "taking it offline," but we only do that if there are some real issues. Otherwise we talk about it right there. There is something special about letting the community police themselves.

There are two things that we talk about at these meetings:

1. **What we did yesterday.** How did you get the previous day's task done? (Or if you didn't, why not?) It's a great way to hold team members accountable for their responsibilities and make them own up to their decisions (good or bad).

2. **Our #1 priority for the day.** In addition to setting
    a goal, we want to know if what we're doing is impact-
    ing somebody else. If someone is waiting for some-
    one else to do something, this is where we communi-
    cate. If everyone stands up and says what they're
    doing today, there are no miscommunications.

What does the standup meeting solve? It eliminates any
back talking and blaming others because you have to answer to your herd. The whole community has a right to
hear why you didn't get something done. There's no back
door. There's no "Oh well, Sandy needs to get this done
first." You have to tell everyone every day what you did
and what you didn't do. It allows the community to work
together towards completion, as opposed to getting lost.
A company can do daily standups until they have around
20 workers, at which point it's more time-efficient to
break the meeting up into two teams.

That's our style of leadership: The execution style. It's
leading in a way that enables the team to consistently
get something done. When your company gets that and
believes in that perspective, your productivity starts to
set you apart from your competitors. Your standard becomes your own, not the national or average standard.

How to Implement Processes and Systems in Your Company

1. **Develop the right mindset.** For a business to
    be a business and not a company of one, the owner
    has to be invested in systems and processes that set
    his or her team up for success.

2. **Read a few books about the mentality of systems.** I would recommend everyone read *Work the System* by Sam Carpenter. I would also read *Checklist Manifesto* by Atul Gawande. You need to have a proper foundation as to *why* your systems work the way they do.

3. **Have your team members write out what they actually do every day.** Don't just build on the job description; have them write you a letter giving you the specifics of their day-to-day tasks.

4. **Number everything in there that's an action.** For everyone's letter to me, I would be able to come up with 1–35 action items that they do in their job.

5. **Identify the things in the person's job that require consistency of a product or service we deliver to a customer.** These should be prioritized at the top.

6. **Have that person create how-you-do-that checklist for each action on the list.** If someone else completes the task, this original person has to sign off on the checklist.

Here are a few more things to keep in mind as you start creating these processes and systems in your business.

Check Your Foundation

Stop right now and ask yourself this question: "Do I believe in superior systems and average people, or great people and inferior systems?" Which do you inherently believe in? While there is not a universally right answer, it is critical to know where you stand on the matter. It's important to how you implement systems.

For me personally, I would always rather have great people in an inferior system. The way I see it, if you develop a great system and then go hire inferior people, you're inherently going to have a system that can't be maintained. I like to say, "The best thing you can give a great person is a good system." When you do that, you're giving them the freedom to thrive beyond what they're capable of right now. The minute you give a great person consistency and structure, they will excel.

It always comes back to people, and if you're keeping inferior people in your system then your system will never work as well as you hoped. Because of that, you're always going to think you're one system away from being a better company.

Some companies have managers in place who are there just to make sure people do their jobs, which means you believe more in a system than you do in people. It's just inherent in that type of mindset. That's not a system that works and it's not what great companies are built on.

The outliers, the people who don't want to support your mission or are mediocre, have to go. You either help them adjust or you have to help them leave because they're just dead weight slowing down your business. You're not doing them any favor by avoiding a difficult conversation, and you're certainly doing your environment or your customer any favors keeping them around. For the rest of my career I will continue to have very painful discussions with wonderfully competent, qualified people who don't belong in our system or in the systems of our client's businesses.

Start With Revenue

I have a "revenue first" mentality in my company. You can dress me up but you can't take the salesman out of me. I am very careful about making sure that bureaucracy doesn't win over customer engagement. And when left to my own devices, the only way I do that is to pay attention to revenue before anything else. It's no surprise then that Shirley and I started our work there.

We started by putting systems in place for our revenue-producing departments because it was the fastest way to impact relationship with our customers (while also freeing my time and attention for other things). Then we worked our way into internal department stuff, like payroll, which were far easier to implement.

Some people have not recognized that you've got to start with the hard things first and then work towards the easier things. It's a fear of failure thing, and it has to go. If you can't overcome that fear then maybe you're better off starting with the easier stuff. It's better to keep executing. I can't say it enough: progress over perfection.

Create New Habits

It takes work and time to create a new habit. We don't even think a habit happens until 30 or 60 days because you have to consistently do it.

First 10 Days: That first 10 days are really tough and everyone wants to fight you. It takes a lot of effort to fight the urge to give up.

Days 10-20: The next 10 days are hard, but easier than the first ten. The urge to quit is still there, but it's easier to move past it.

Days 20+: When you get to the third set of ten days, you start to feel some euphoria. It's a time where you actually feel like this is the right thing to do. The third set of ten days is critical to a business.

Now imagine having to recreate that attitude over and over and over for three months as more and more people start their 30 to 60-day habit-creating cycles. It's not easy. It's just consistent.

We took the most overwhelming part out (this idea that we've never done this before and it needs to be perfect) and reduced it to a very simple approach. We went to one place at a time and got each team member heavily involved in his or her piece of the process.

Changing Processes and Systems

The flexibility and freedom to be able to tweak processes and systems is critical. If a team member doesn't feel like they have a part in the process, we've lost the whole point. If making your job easier is about you then we don't care. If making your job more efficient is better for the client, then we will support it in two seconds. We absolutely want consistency, but if you can see a better way to serve the client then that's fine.

If a process doesn't work because it's impacting the delivery or consistency to the client, then not only do we embrace changing it but we also make sure that it gets passed down and we improve the process for everybody.

That happened in our business recently. Our clients have their own unique login to access their financials. We had that hosted in a cloud and because of security concerns we required our clients to log in through specific systems to do any work. It was smart, it was good, and it was necessary for the protection of clients' information. It just wasn't efficient.

What was actually happening was that people were not installing the apps in our environment. They were literally duplicating their effort to adhere to our system. Finally one of our people stopped and said, "Hey, has anyone considered why we do this? I think we can do one less step and still get this done." We discovered that we could use a direct login into our cloud and support a local environment. We cut 20 to 30 minutes of waste out of everyone's job because someone questioned a system we had put in place.

The change ultimately resulted in the client having a better turnaround on delivery. It didn't translate into the client's bill getting smaller. It didn't translate into the employees' jobs getting easier. It translated into us delivering a measurably better and more consistent service because we weren't wasting our time.

That's why we want people being change agents within our company. We don't want to follow one set system because the system is designed to deliver the best product and consistent service to the customer. Our rule is: If you discover something that isn't the best product, then we need to fix it. That's why it's ever moving and ever flowing, and that's why I always say the best brands know this and live it.

Job Descriptions

Your team members' job descriptions need to be built on two principles:

1.   The core values of your company
2.   The detail of the job that person has to do.

The job description should only be one page long, with very clear directives. If it can't be set on one page then you don't know what it's talking about. Simpler is better.

Interviews

I often sit in and audit my client business owner's job candidate interviews. Invariably, there's no job description sitting there. The candidate has never even seen a full job description. This is a huge mistake. There are three reasons why you should at least have the job description at the interview, if not before.

- **The job description is a tool to help put in the right people and weed out the wrong ones.** If I were a candidate who hadn't seen the job description, I would be spending all my energy and time in the interview trying to layout the vision for the job. In reality, all the company had to do before the interview is mail over the job description to find out if I was interested. If I don't want the job, I won't waste anyone's time with an interview

- **It'll provide clarity.** If the candidate asks something about the job description, you can say, "did you read that or do you want to go back over that? Here's what the core job is."

- **It allows you to strengthen your vision of the employee you want.** Do you remember what is supposed to happen in an interview? You, as the leader, need to spend all my time evaluating effort, ability, and attitude, not describing the job.

We use job descriptions as these stagnant things, but in reality there should be a little bit of fluidity. If we are replacing someone that has left the team we don't have reinvent the job description, but it might be smart to re-evaluate some of the finer points using our experience with the previous employee. There are often improvements to be made because the job took on another meaning actually during its life to that point.

Team Members

After a new employee starts working, there's an important question you should ask:

"Now that you've been in the company, tell us what your job description should be based on your talent and skills. What do you think you should be doing as a job, and what part of that are you not doing now?"

This is kind of an assessment we put the job description through. We look at our job description and ask, "Is it right for our mission and core values? Is it working? Or do we just stick to this thing we printed out and check we got job description done?"

A job description, like any system, has to be agile and it has to be reviewed. What happens is over time we start wondering what happened to the infamous Rachel. What happened to Rachel when we started giving her more to do and her performance waned? We lost sight of what she should have been doing. If we've added to things to their plate that are hurting their performance, then we need to get that off their plate.

That's why job descriptions are critical for us. They start with foundational hiring and become a road map to make sure our people are positioned correctly.

Quarterly Cleanups

The only way you can find out some of that stuff is by talking directly to your employees. At Fully Account-

Final Word

So there you have it...

If there's one thing I hope you take from this book it's that, as an owner or CEO, you can't concentrate your talents and expertise on a sole facet of your company — tempting as it may be, and, expect to thrive and grow your business to the next level.

The CEO's mind has to be comprehensive. It has to account for all six critical areas of his or her company:

1. Your Mindset
2. Your Team
3. The Real Numbers
4. Great Products & Services
5. Sales Message & Proper Marketing Channels
6. The Systems and Processes

In order to do this (and to do it well), the CEO's mindset must be focused on a clearly defined mission and driven toward execution. It must be committed to building the best version of every product or service, and working to continually improve it. The CEO's mindset must be set on finding the right people for the team, and working to ensure everyone is in the right place. It means focusing on the aspects of sales and marketing that are most important rather than getting bogged down with every last detail at the expense of everything else. It means establishing reports to enable data-driven decisions and putting good financial measures in place to catch issues before they turn into problems. And it means creating the proper systems in each area of the company in order to keep it running smoothly and consistently delivering value to the customer.

If you take the time now to invest in yourself, change your mindset, and focus on the tools and techniques to develop an Execution Attitude in your entire company, you will realize growth, profit and happiness that you originally set out to achieve.

Where to go from here:

1. Change Your Mindset

I would encourage you to look at the changes that you need to make to your company *and* your role within it. You need to renew your mind and take on a mindset of growth and execution. You really can do this!

2. Determine Your Mission

Get a clear understanding of your company's mission. Regardless of the age of your company, this is very valuable. A rudderless ship goes nowhere. Take the time to get on mission. You and your company are worth it.

3. Develop an Execution Attitude

You and your team need to develop an attitude of execution first. The power of momentum is unquestioned.

The more work you get done on your goals the more it builds. Having a culture built on results promotes progress.

4. Find Your Heartbeat

In order to grow a truly efficient team, you must know the core values of your heart. "The way it beats!" This will allow you to be surrounded by people who work best with you. It will single handedly change the hiring process and growth of your team!

5. Build Your Team

Growing a team should not be a guess. It should be completely strategic. Identify the holes in the company and hire and train in accordance with your company heartbeat and personality types.

6. Know Your Real Numbers

You must have someone dedicated to the analysis of your real numbers. Tracking your numbers is the most important factor possibly only second to team in thriving as a business.

7. Pave the Dirt Road

We are always starting new things. I am truly okay with that. But in order for process and order to exist in a company, you must develop a mindset of asset building. The structure and process of your company is an asset that will continue to pay into the future. Walking down a dirt road once is okay. We need to have the mindset to pave behind as we move along!

I hope your investment of time reading this book proved valuable. As I suggested in the beginning treat this book as a working manual. Go back and do the suggested exercises. Your life, company, and fulfillment will significantly improve.

Appendix

Footnotes

Preface:

1. Exercises and Resources found at: www.thetotalceo.com/
    mindset. We put a full resource center together to help you
    with the tools for success. But please know without your ef-
    fort the tools will not come alive in your life and business.

Chapter 1: Your Mindset

2. Exercise: Crafting Your Mission. Your mission is a critical
    cornerstone of your business. I hope and pray you take action
    immediately on this.

3. 37 Signals. The owners of a great tool basecamp. Love this
    quote.

4   www.thetotalceo.com/mindset. You can learn more about
    Total CEO's development and processes here.

5. Resources: Identify your talents.www.thetotalceo.com/
    mindset.

6. Resources: Don't forget to create your mission!

    www.thetotalceo.com/mindset.

7. Resources: Learn more about what we're doing!

    www.fullyaccountable.com.

Chapter 2: People

8. Jim Collins. Great Author. I highly encourage you as a busi-
    ness leader to read his books.

9. Finding Your Heartbeat. This exercise will help you figure out your core heartbeat. Critical in proper hiring.

10. Perfect Interview Resource. www.thetotalceo.com/mindest.

11. Paul Graham. Great person to watch on how he evaluates good ideas and people.

12. GTE Motto. I truly resonate with this slogan.

13. Information and Resources on Hiring.

    www.thetotalceo.com/mindset.

14. Jim Jensen. Perfect example and vision of a hybrid. Fun also to remember what he did in my childhood.

15. Dave Ramsey. Financial author and motivational speaker.

16. Access to the Perfect Interview Resource.

    www.thetotalceo.com/mindset.

Chapter 3: Your Real Numbers

17 www.FullyAccountable.com. We offer an outsourced CFO and complete done for you accounting service for the small business ranging in size from 1 million to 25 million in revenue.

18. Sample Metrics Resource. We believe if you have a dedicated person paying attention to the real numbers, you have a significantly greater chance of thriving.

    www.fullyaccountable.com/resources.

    www.thetotalceo.com/mindset.

Chapter 4: Products and Services

19. Facebook Motto. Critical to getting your idea, service, and product into the hands of your consumers.

20. Learning more about product and services resource. This is a critical area of the company where on execution attitude will solve many problems. www.thetotalceo.com/mindset.

Chapter 5: Sales & Marketing

21. Ryan Deiss. Check out my dear friend at

    www.digitalmarketer.com.

22. USP Exercise. Simplicity, clarity, and focus are the ingredients to a winning sales message. This resource will help you and your team on the USP journey

    www.thetotalceo.com/mindset.

Chapter 6: Processes and Systems

23. Steve Wozniak. A good talk helping to remember the value of structure and consistency.

24. *Checklist Manifesto.* A must read for integration and the people who are in charge of the structure.

25. *Work the System.* Once you decide that systems are important, this book will help with a map.

26. Execution Attitude Resource. www.thetotalceo.com/mindset.

27. The Best Investment: A Better You. This is my first book. It was a true passion project. It will help you discover your true gifts and how to offer value with those gifts to others.

    www.abetteryou.com.

Exercise Recap

Resources/Exercises:

Chapter 1:

Exercise One: Crafting Your Mission

Go to www.thetotalceo.com/mindset to access our mission creation documents.

Clear away two hours and commit to writing down your core service(s)/product(s) and what you want to accomplish.

Resources:

1. **Identify your talents.** We have exercises posted at www.thetotalceo.com/mindset.

2. **Don't forget to create your mission!** You can find Fully Accountable's™ mission statement at www.thetotalceo.com/mindset.

3. **Learn more about what we're doing!** You can learn more about Fully Accountable™ at www.fully-accountable.com.

Chapter 2:

Finding Your Heartbeat!

1. Write down between 10-15 values that describe you and your executive team (if it's just you, that's fine). No need to define them yet. Just write the words.

2. Share those terms with your executive team and ask them each to pick five from the list. Also allow them to have a write-in if they feel strongly about anything that is not on the list. Be sure to pick your own five as well.

3. Meet with the executive team and have each person state their five terms plus their reasons for selecting them.

4. Compile the list, confirm the ones you all agree upon, and work through any disagreement until you mutually agree on your company's five core values.

Exercise: Sit down and think about what you're not good at, what you want to accomplish, and why you should add someone to the team to accomplish the task. Prioritize the list based on the most important holes for that season of your business.

Chapter 3:

DIY Metrics- Quick Exercise to Figure Out KPIs

If you want to put a system in place by yourself, I would recommend you follow these three steps:

1. Figure out which key metrics are important for your business.

2. Find a way to look at your key performance indicators. This can be as simple as an excel file or as complex as a dashboard software.

3. Hire somebody who can dedicate their day to monitoring and reporting on key metrics. This is the most important part.

Chapter 5:

Exercise: Take a blank piece of paper and write out your mission for the company. Even if you had one originally, write one now and see what it looks like for this season of your company. Sit with your team and work on revising it to a simple one-sentence (two at maximum) message.

Acknowledgments

Writing this book took more time, effort and resources than I originally expected. I would like to first thank God for giving me the wisdom to pull together the content of this book and for having the perseverance to complete it;

I would like to thank my wife Debbi for being my best friend and putting up with the long hours and time commitment to make this project come alive. I am also truly thankful for her and how great she is as my wife and the mother of our four children;

I would like to thank my four children: Sophia, Vinny, Jacob and Elizabeth for honoring their mom and dad. And I also love that each one of them are significant contributors to our family and our figuring out how to love and help others daily;

I would like to thank my dear friend Jeff who is always so graceful in his critique of my work. I also appreciate how God has used him to push me on making sure truth is best represented at all times.

I would to thank my team Rachel, Devon, Ashley, and all of the other team members who helped make this book come alive.

I would like to thank my friend Ed, who is always helping me see the big picture and keeping the energy positive;

I would like to thank Hubert for being a good friend who pushes me to think differently;

I would like to thank Tony for being an amazing friend who is humble, gracious, and so giving. He is always lifting me up.

I would like to thank Ann and her team for helping to edit my book and make the finished product so much better;

I would also like to thank each person not specifically named in this letter for any help or assistance you gave me in bringing this book to life. I am truly thankful for having a strong network of people in my life who care and are committed to my success; and

Finally, I am thankful for you the reader who took the investment to read this book. Your lives will be positively impacted by its content. I pray that it's as helpful to you as it has been for me in my life.

Thank you for reading!

I hope you enjoyed *The CEO's Mindset: How to Break Through to the Next Level*. I felt so compelled to share my message and help as many entrepreneur CEO's understand the value being a of complete leadership.

This is my first business book, so I'd love to get your feedback on it. I'd love to know what you think.

If you could take a few minutes to leave a review of this book on Amazon, I would really appreciate it! For instructions on how to leave your review, just visit http://theceosmindset.com/leave-a-review/.

I truly value your feedback, and I can't wait to hear from you!

In gratitude,

Vinnie Fisher

About the Author

Vinnie Fisher is a businessman, entrepreneur, author, husband, and father. He has been married for almost 20 years to his wife Debbi, and together they have four children: Sophia, Vinny, Jacob, and Elizabeth.

A lawyer by trade, Vinnie practiced tax and business law for 10 years before leaving the field in 2007 to pursue entrepreneurship full-time. His first venture, Creative Learning Workshop, provides day habilitation and vocational services to adults with developmental disabilities. Vinnie sold the business in 2009, after opening nine locations in Ohio and providing many of new jobs for Ohio residents.

In 2007, Vinnie also started his first of many Internet-based businesses, an information publishing company that taught clients how to start, grow, and maintain their own successful work-from-home businesses. Vinnie sold the business in 2010, and that same year opened the first of a suite of web hosting companies.

By the summer of 2014, Vinnie had caught the entrepreneurial bug again and opened Fully Accountable™, a full-service accounting firm that provides outsourced CFO and a full service accounting back office solution for small and medium closely held businesses ranging from 1 million to 25 million in revenue. What makes

Fully Accountable™ truly unique is that their team doesn't just prepare clients' financial reports—they actually review and analyze their reports and send clients daily, actionable feedback on what they need to know about their business. It's that unique selling proposition that has skyrocketed Fully Accountable's™ growth in an amazingly short period of time. Vinnie currently serves as Chairman of the Board and Chief Visionary for the business.

And as if 2014 wasn't a busy enough year already, at the end of the year Vinnie wrote this first book, The Best Investment: A Better You and opened his publishing company, A Better You Publishing.[27]

In late 2015, Vinnie and his team launched Total CEO (www.thetotalceo.com). Vinnie is the co-founder and chief visionary of Total CEO. His mission is to help untrap entrepreneurs from certain operations of the business and allow them to get back to their dreams that launched their company in the first place.

You can learn more about the author at

www.Vinniefisher.com.

Do you know an entrepreneur, business owner, CEO
or friend trying to Break Through to the Next Level?

Purchase a bulk order to help others establish
The CEO's Mindset

ORDER HERE:
www.theceosmindset.com/bulkorder

Best-Selling Author Of:

The Best Investment
A BETTER YOU
Now Available on amazon.com